W9-CKL-833

Books by Carvel Collins

THE AMERICAN SPORTING GALLERY
LITERATURE IN THE MODERN WORLD (With Others)

Editor

FRANK NORRIS: *McTeague* (RINEHART EDITION)
WILLIAM FAULKNER: NEW ORLEANS SKETCHES
WILLIAM FAULKNER: *The Unvanquished*
(SIGNET CLASSICS EDITION)
ERSKINE CALDWELL'S MEN AND WOMEN
FAULKNER'S UNIVERSITY PIECES
WILLIAM FAULKNER: EARLY PROSE AND POETRY

William Faulkner:
Early Prose and Poetry

[signature]

William Faulkner:
Early Prose and Poetry

*"Faulkner House"
Pirate's Alley
New
Orleans
where
W. F. lived
& wrote
1994*

Compilation and Introduction

by

CARVEL COLLINS

WITH ILLUSTRATIONS

EAST CAMDEN

An Atlantic Monthly Press Book
LITTLE, BROWN AND COMPANY · BOSTON · TORONTO

Ja 17 '63

2.62
Ward

COPYRIGHT © 1962 BY CARVEL COLLINS

ALL RIGHTS RESERVED. NO PART OF THIS BOOK MAY BE REPRO-
DUCED IN ANY FORM WITHOUT PERMISSION IN WRITING FROM THE
PUBLISHER, EXCEPT BY A REVIEWER WHO MAY QUOTE BRIEF PAS-
SAGES IN A REVIEW TO BE PRINTED IN A MAGAZINE OR NEWSPAPER.

LIBRARY OF CONGRESS CATALOG CARD NO. 62–17953

FIRST EDITION

63 - 220

ATLANTIC—LITTLE, BROWN BOOKS
ARE PUBLISHED BY
LITTLE, BROWN AND COMPANY
IN ASSOCIATION WITH
THE ATLANTIC MONTHLY PRESS

Published simultaneously in Canada
by Little, Brown & Company (Canada) Limited

PRINTED IN THE UNITED STATES OF AMERICA

To
the amiable members of
the Faulkner Seminar,
University of Tokyo, 1961-62,
the compilation of this volume
is warmly dedicated.

Preface

WILLIAM FAULKNER added to his already growing reputation in Japan when he took part in the seminar of university teachers and students held at Nagano in 1955. Strongly impressed by him, members of that seminar have said they doubt they will ever again experience such an incandescent meeting. And younger Japanese students have volunteered that they not only admire Faulkner's fiction but would like to thank him for the address he wrote "To the Youth of Japan."

Now that Faulkner is again the subject of study by a seminar of students and teachers in Japan, at the University of Tokyo, it is pleasant to present to them in this volume some of the work he produced forty years ago while he himself was part of a university community.

When Faulkner's University of Mississippi poetry, prose, and drawings first came to the compiler's knowledge, it seemed well not to reprint such early work. His great, mature books had not yet won him the Nobel Prize; and though readers were admiring them in increasing numbers, many critics still held them in low regard. But now, widely recognized as a major world writer, Faulkner has such stature that even his earliest works are of interest to many. So it no longer seems helpful to postpone reprinting such pieces. And it seems well to reprint them now in the hope of avoiding confusion like that which a few years ago accompanied the reprinting of Faulkner's early New Orleans newspaper sketches: During the same year in which the compiler came upon and postponed reprinting these University of Mississippi pieces he came upon those New Orleans sketches and thought it best also to postpone reprinting them, for the same reason. But within a short time other admirers of Faulkner published eleven of the sixteen New Orleans sketches and later, after hearing about two more of them, published a second volume containing just those two sketches. It then seemed proper to bring out the complete set of sixteen New Orleans sketches — and that postponing their reprinting had clearly not been a service to Faulkner studies after all. The situation has begun to repeat itself with Faulkner's University of Mississippi pieces: most of them have been found and several projects for publishing them are planned by scholars who have not come upon all the materials reprinted here, already a few of the drawings have been reproduced, parts of the prose have been quoted in articles, and an article in an anthology of college writing has reprinted part of the poems. So, with close students of Faulkner here and elsewhere becoming interested in his early writings, it seems well to publish this little compilation now to honor both Faulkner's effectiveness at Nagano and the enthusiasm of the members of the current University of Tokyo seminar.

The many people whose reminiscences, advice, and general assistance have made possible the gathering of these and similar materials already know the compiler's full awareness of the debt he owes them, which he looks forward to acknowledging in detail elsewhere. Here he wants to take the opportunity to thank those who supplied the documents, sanctions, and professional services on which this little compilation immediately depends: the staffs of *The Mississippian* newspaper and the *Ole Miss* annual for their generosity and cooperation; Mr. George W. Healey, Jr., and the late Dr. Raymond B. Zeller, former Editors of *The Scream,* and Mr. Branham Hume, former Business Manager of that magazine, for their support and open-handed offering of drawings and details of publishing history; Dr. Leon Picon of the United States Embassy here, who contributed so much in 1955 to the success of the Nagano seminar, for information and advice; Mrs. John Pilkington for her generous and efficient checking of Mississippi documents; the staffs of the libraries at the University of Mississippi, the Massachusetts Institute of Technology, the University of Texas, Harvard University, and Yale University for assistance of many kinds; the staff of the Microreproduction Laboratory at M.I.T. for reproductions of illustrations and for skillful photographic salvaging of burned manuscript pages; the staff of the office which registers the deeds of Lafayette County, Mississippi, for unflagging patience during the examination of their file of Oxford newspapers; as well as the staff of the Oxford *Eagle* for assistance far beyond the call of hospitality. And because it has been a pleasure to assemble this little volume, from materials brought to Japan as seminar illustrations with no thought of publishing them as a book, the compiler wants to thank those Japanese students who urged its publication out of their admiration for William Faulkner.

Tokyo, 1961

Preface to the American Edition

THESE EARLY published works by William Faulkner having been made available to Japanese readers because of a seminar offered at the University of Tokyo, it has been suggested that they be made available to Americans interested in Faulkner's writing. This edition expands the Japanese volume by adding photographs and "Portrait," the poem which Faulkner published in the New Orleans *Double Dealer* during 1922 while he was still at the University of Mississippi. The appendix added to this edition contains four works which Faulkner published in the same literary magazine in 1925 shortly after leaving the University for New Orleans: two critical essays which bear on his University writings, and two poems — "Dying Gladiator" and "The Faun" — which he published before his first novel and which are not included among the poems he later collected in *A Green Bough*. Though these two essays and three poems from the *Double Dealer* were among the items reprinted in 1932 by Paul Romaine in his *Salmagundi,* that volume is unfortunately out of print. The compiler and the publishers want to express their gratitude to Mrs. Lillian Friend Marcus, Managing Editor of the *Double Dealer,* for her permission to reprint here these additional works of early prose and poetry by William Faulkner.

Cambridge, Massachusetts, 1962

Contents

William Faulkner:
Early Prose and Poetry

Faulkner at
the University of Mississippi

WILLIAM FAULKNER drew a picture for the 1916-1917 annual of the University of Mississippi. It began a series of contributions he was to make during the next eight years to that annual, to the University newspaper, and to a University humor magazine. By 1925 these three publications had brought out at least sixteen more of his drawings, sixteen of his poems, his first published short story and prose sketch, and six of his reviews and literary articles — the artistic explorations of a young man who would become the best novelist his country has produced in this century.

Faulkner's father, an officer in the administration of the University of Mississippi, which adjoins the town of Oxford, had a house on its campus, in which William Faulkner lived for much of the period under discussion here. In such close physical association with the University he found its publications open to him not only during the time he was enrolled as a student but earlier when he worked at a bank and later when he ran the University Post Office.

A former student of that era has kindly volunteered his memory that Faulkner wrote in 1916 for the University's newspaper two or three imitation "Letters of a Japanese School Boy" which were his earliest publications. A series of such letters did appear; but at its conclusion the newspaper identified its author as another man, and there seems to be little possibility of attributing individual letters from that series to Faulkner. It seems equally impossible to attribute to him with any certainty another, shorter series of imitation letters of the same period, though he may have written some of them. Even high school publications as yet unavailable may contain written juvenilia or drawings similar to ten of Faulkner's pen-and-ink school sketches which survive from 1913. But his first published work which this investigation has been able to identify is the signed drawing for the 1916-1917 *Ole Miss* annual.

It was followed the next year by two signed drawings in the 1917-1918 *Ole Miss,* one of them for the same "Social Activities" page his first had decorated, the other to decorate a page listing the members of a dancing group. Faulkner presumably supplied the staff of *Ole Miss* with these drawings before April 10, 1918; for on that day he began work as a ledger clerk at an armament company in Connecticut. Signing up with the Royal Flying Corps, and then resigning from his job as clerk on June 15, 1918, he made a brief trip home to visit his family before leaving Mississippi on July 8, 1918, for Toronto, Canada, to begin training as a pilot. Four months later came the Armistice. When the British re-

WILLIAM FAULKNER IN 1918, AS A CADET IN THE
ROYAL FLYING CORPS, TRAINING IN CANADA

leased him from training the following month, he returned from Canada to Mississippi.

That spring and summer — according to Phil Stone, a close associate of those days — Faulkner did even more reading than usual and wrote much of the poetry he would revise for *The Marble Faun* of five years later. On August 6, 1919, *The New Republic* printed his poem "L'Apres-Midi d'un Faune," his first piece of writing known to have been published and his first published draft on the Symbolist poets from whom he would draw so much. At summer's end, on September 19, 1919, he registered as a student at the University of Mississippi, enrolling in French, Spanish, and the sophomore survey of English literature.

His first contributions to the University's newspaper, *The Mississippian,* were a slightly revised version of "L'Apres-Midi d'un Faune" in October and, on November 12, 1919, the poem "Cathay." "Cathay" illustrates some of the uncertainties which accompany reprinting these pieces: Lines of the poem in *The Mississippian* seem to have been disturbed by faulty typesetting, but perfect guidance for emendation is not to be found in the other three available versions. The most accessible of the three is a typescript William Faulkner loaned to the Princeton University Library for its exhibition of 1957, which now can be seen as Plate 3 among the illustrations in James B. Meriwether's excellent book *The Literary Career of William Faulkner* (Princeton, 1961). It differs from the printed version at points where *The Mississip-*

pian seems not to have made typographical errors. The other two versions came to light about a decade after a 1941 fire had destroyed a house containing early Faulkner papers — when I was able, with the kind consent and help of the owners, to separate from the debris, dry out, and read more than four hundred and seventy pages, including a damaged holograph version of this poem dated 1920 and an undated, damaged typescript of it. They differ at several points not only from the version in *The Mississippian* but from the version Mr. Faulkner loaned to Princeton. These documents differ because William Faulkner revised and improved his early poems for several years, printing some of them as late as 1933, after he not only had become a novelist but had created that fictional masterpiece, *The Sound and the Fury*.

The Mississippian launched Faulkner as an author of fiction two weeks after it had printed his poem "Cathay," when it brought out on November 26, 1919, the first story he is known to have published, titled "Landing in Luck" and set at a military training aerodrome in Canada.

In the same issue the newspaper published another of his poems, "Sapphics," and in subsequent issues during the rest of that 1919-1920 academic year published ten more. Most of them were more sophisticated than the verse other students wrote for the newspaper, and the discrepancy created opposition to Faulkner's work. On February 4, 1920, the week after he published "Une

Ballade des Femmes Perdues," a fellow student parodied it. After Faulkner published "Naiads' Song" and "Fantoches," which the paper mis-set as "Fantouches," the parodist struck again, with "Whotouches," signed "J." As an artist partly apprenticed to the Symbolists, Faulkner already must have learned from them to expect hostility of this sort; and one would like to imagine that, while he was learning to adapt to his own circumstances and skills some of the aesthetic practice and theory of the authors of *"L'Après-midi d'un Faune"* and *"Fantoches,"* Faulkner was also learning from *les poètes maudits* to cherish more and more the natural independence and self-containment within which he has recorded his aesthetic perceptions with remarkable indifference to much neglect and hostility during long early years, great adulation during recent years, and considerable misunderstanding throughout.

With his "Fantoches," on February 25, 1920, Faulkner began the publication of a group of four poems which he specifically connected with their source, in this case the work of Paul Verlaine. "Clair de Lune," the second of this group of four — all of them using Verlaine's titles — appeared on March 3, 1920, and the third, "Streets," on March 17. Faulkner's adaptation of Verlaine's "Streets" was not his only contribution to that issue of *The Mississippian;* in addition to a poem called "A Poplar" he published one of the very few responses he has ever made to the reactions of his readers, a reply to the student "J" who had parodied two of his earlier poems. Appearing under the title "The Ivory Tower," this reply said (in part and with the obvious typographical errors removed):

Ben Jonson, himself a strong advocate of Mirth, has said that laughter is one of our most valuable possessions. Which is quite true: Imagine what this world would be without it. Yet mirth requires two things: humor and a sense of humor. I flatter myself that I possess the latter; but — and I am sure I am unprejudiced — my unknown "affinity" has notably failed in producing the former. I will state further, that in his present vein he will never achieve it without asking — and accepting — collaboration. It were not sufficient that I boldly make this statement lest the reader justifiably cry "Wolf!"; yet the matter is scarcely worth exhausting either my vocabulary or the reader's patience, so I shall be as brief as possible.

(1.) The first poem submitted by him was stupid, for my own poem was stupid. One sees at a glance then, the utter valuelessness of an imitation of an imitation. (2.) This though, was not the only way in which the poet sinned. The most deplorable thing was his meaningless and unnecessary parading of his doubtless extensive knowledge of the Latin language. To my mind there is nothing as vulgar as a conscious mingling of two languages — unless, of course, the mingling gives shades and tones that the work would not otherwise possess. Whatever tones and shades his poem possessed could have, it seems to me, been drawn in single language (its clarity could have been enhanced, in all probability, by adhering to some simple language such as an early Aztec dialect). This though, is beside the point.

The second poem is not worthy of note, closely resembling the first in being a vulgarly stupid agglomeration of words. . . . if this be humor, then I have lost my sense of it; unless humor is, like evil, in the eye of the beholder.

[*9*]

However, if he has, by any chance, gained the effect for which he has so palpably striven, the answer is, of course, simply de gustibus.

William Falkner.

Faulkner, in signing this response, followed the form of his family name which his father, grandfather, and great-grandfather used, as he did in signing most of his University of Mississippi pieces which are reprinted here. Discussions of who put the "u" in William Faulkner's name rival in number the renditions of that great musical question about the overalls in Mrs. Murphy's chowder. Insignificant as the matter is, the continual confusion concerning it illustrates the immaturity of much writing about Faulkner. The customary — and wrong — explanation of the change in spelling is one of the small counterfeit coins which too many workers in the Faulkner industry have passed among themselves from the beginning to the present. For example, the most recent of the American books of Faulkner criticism, Frederick J. Hoffman, *William Faulkner* (New York, 1961), referring to the year 1924 in its "Chronology," says, "First book published: *The Marble Faun,* a book of poems, published by the Four Seas Co. of Boston. Because of printer's error, a "u" added to Faulkner's name, which he has retained." That is as untrue as an even less interesting piece of this minor coinage which once again reappears in another recent, small book, Michael Millgate, *William Faulkner* (Edinburgh, 1961): that in the First World War, as Millgate puts it, Faulkner "managed to join the Canadian Flying Corps," which must have taken considerable managing because in that war Canada had no air force. These bits of biographical counterfeit, of course, have no importance whatever. But when such tertiary books, drawing them from dubious secondary sources, offer them again and again, they are an obvious reminder of the existence of a more subtle, much more significant false coinage of critical judgment which such books also circulate. The "u" in Faulkner's name began to appear intermittently some years before the publication of *The Marble Faun* in 1924 by printers to whose error the spelling is continually attributed. According to the staff of the armament company for which Faulkner worked in Connecticut from April into June of 1918, his name appears in their records of that year's employees as "William Faulkner." His first known published literary work signed "Faulkner" is his first known published literary work: "L'Apres-Midi d'un Faune," *New Republic,* 1919. To reduce the possibility that writers on Faulkner will attribute that insertion of the "u" — more than five years before the publication of *The Marble Faun* — to an error by the *New Republic* printers, it may be well to mention other early appearances of "Faulkner." Among the burned sheets of his early writings salvaged some years ago was a small, badly damaged, beautifully produced booklet of poems, hand-lettered as a gift to a friend, titled *The Lilacs,* dated January 1, 1920, and bearing, carefully lettered by its author, the name "W. Faulkner." One of the two copies I have read of the booklet titled *Marionettes,* which Faulkner "published" himself in pen-and-ink and circulated to a few

WILLIAM FAULKNER IN THE UNIFORM
OF THE BRITISH AIR FORCE

friends, bears the date "1920" and the name "W. Faulkner," both in Faulkner's characteristic lettering. In addition to his booklet *The Lilacs,* other items among the fire-damaged papers of his University of Mississippi years which relate to this little matter are typescripts of poems by "William Faulkner" which bear dates earlier than that of *The Marble Faun.* So, apparently, this is one puzzling spelling printers did not cause, and the answer to the question Who Put the "u" in William Faulkner's Name? is William Falkner.

Whatever way he was spelling his family name, Faulkner's importing to the Mississippi campus not only the works of French Symbolists but a walking stick; his detached air of unemployment which masked his dedication to the labor of writing, which has produced more than twenty-five books and was already producing the formative published and unpublished pieces of those early years; and his awareness, common to uncommon genius, that he would one day become a first-rate artist — all these had led some of the college students to give him the nickname "Count," which the student "J" used in a letter printed in *The Mississippian* for March 24, 1920. This is apparently the first published commentary on Faulkner's works — and one more similar in tone to many of the commentaries on Faulkner published before the Second World War than it is pleasant to recollect:

I feel it my duty to answer an article that appeared in the last issue of your very estimable paper. This article seems to have been written by a peculiar person who calls himself

William Falkner and who from all accounts undoubtedly resides in the remote village of Oxford, Miss. He says he "flatters" himself that he possesses a sense of humor. I say he flatters himself if he says he possesses anything. "I boldly make this statement lest the Editor justifiably cry 'Bull.' " I shall, of course, make this article very brief, desiring to conserve the valuable space in this paper and also my own exhaustible energy for some more serious subject.

I feel, Mr. Editor, like kicking myself three successive times, each a trifle severer than the former. I tried so hard to find what the Count was "driving at," and only that he, himself, admits his work was "stupid." Modesty forbids me using a stronger epithet than "stupid."

I have written the parodies to give Count's poems a meaning; and behold! how little he appreciates my humble efforts.

But permit me to wander. Mr. Editor, wouldn't this be a fine University if all of us were to wear sailor collars, monkey hats, and brilliant pantaloons; if we would 'mose' along the street by the aid of a walking prop; and, ye gods forbid, if we should while away our time singing of lascivious knees, smiling lute strings, and voluptuous toes? Wouldn't that be just too grand?

Since Count used a quotation, allow me the same liberty. I use the words of Lord Byron, "He brays, the Laureate of the long-eared kind."

And now, allow me to apologize for wasting your valuable time on such a subject, and permit me to remain,

Your humble servant,

— J.

Two weeks later the controversy in *The Mississippian* over Faulkner's poetry had not abated, for the paper carried a brief note by Faulkner wondering of "J" "where did he learn English construction?" and a lengthy defense of Faulkner by someone signing himself "F," a new participant in the controversy who seems now to our hindsight pleasantly perceptive:

I feel it my duty to answer an article that appeared in the last issue of your very estimable paper. This article seems to have been written by a peculiar person who signs himself "J" . . .

I think some gentle reader should undertake to defend Count in this controversy. Of all the by-products of nature, a poet is the least able to protect himself in such a dilemma. . . .

It is not intended to infer that Count could not answer this article as well as anyone else. However, he is probably now, in his fancy, with the keen discernment of a poetic eye, measuring the dimple on the knee of some fairy, figuratively speaking, so that he can convey to our thirsting souls in rhythmic verse its full significance. Rather than have him interrupted in this, I burden my weak shoulders with the task, and for once in my life perhaps place nobility under obligations to me.

"J" 's following Count's passionate outbursts with some of his Possum Hollow poetry adds about as much dignity and calm to the majestic pose and sweep of Count's literary course as a tomato can tied to a poodle's tail. . . .

The only excuse he has for this propensity to pester the poets seems to be that he is giving them meaning. Ha! well might one use a raindrop to measure the ocean's depth, choose the movement of a turtle to explain the eagle's flight, or listen to the screech of the "J" bird to interpret the love notes of a dove.

Poets don't sprout in every garden of learning, and how can they grow and bloom into a genius when they are continually surrounded by bitterweeds. . . .

This defense of Faulkner's poetry ended the controversy with "J" except for a weak letter which "J" published almost a month later, on May 5, saying he had delayed his reply on the assumption that Faulkner's defender "had been shipped to Jackson for treatment" in the state insane asylum. *The Mississippian* published only two more parodies of Faulkner's poetry, apparently by new performers: in the same issue which contained the letter from "F," a parody of Faulkner's "Clair de Lune," titled "Cane de Looney"; and during the next month, on May 12, a parody of his "Une Ballade des Femmes Perdues," titled "Une Ballade d'une Vache Perdue," execrably written but briefly arresting because of its crude presentation of a motif which Faulkner himself would use for humor in a piece first published in French translation during 1943 as *"L'Après-midi d'une Vache"* and which he would use for thematic point, parody, and pathos as well as humor in *The Hamlet* when the idiot wanders with his cow. Though the parodies ended and though Faulkner received visible support of his writing — in addition to that in the letter by "F" — when he won a prize for the best literary work in the 1920 *Mississippian,* a fellow student and good friend recalls that Faulkner's departure from campus poetic convention led to his being blackballed for membership in a literary society — a vote amusing to Faulkner's friend, and others.

On April 14 *The Mississippian* published "A Clymène," the last of the four poems which Faulkner ascribed to Verlaine. With "Study," on April 21, 1920, and "Alma Mater," on May 12, *The Mississippian* concluded its publication of works by Faulkner during his first year as a student. But his University productions of that year were not over: the 1919-1920 *Ole Miss* in its end-of-year appearance contained six of his pieces, five of them drawings. Faulkner had served during the college year as one of the art editors on the staff under the writer Louis Cochran, who was then a student and the annual's editor in chief. In addition to Faulkner's drawings, the annual also contained his poem "To a Co-ed," which Cochran had invited him to contribute — and which has led Cochran to joke about having been the first publisher to get Faulkner's writing into a book.

The next autumn, when Faulkner again enrolled at the University, he joined at once in formally founding the Marionettes as the University's official dramatic society. Faulkner's friend Ben Wasson, whose work later appeared on Broadway, was the first president; and Faulkner was in charge of staging the plays, such as *The Arrival of Kitty,* performed the next January. Members of the Marionettes recall that several of them, including Faulkner, had enjoyed producing plays for a year or more before officially connecting their group with the University, and Faulkner was to continue with the society for some years beyond his semesters as a student, being an honorary member until 1925.

Early in his association with the Marionettes, Faulkner wrote a one-act play titled *Marionette*s, which he "published" for friends as a few attractive hand-lettered booklets. The first page of the text of one copy and its facing drawing have been made generally accessible as Figure 1 of the illustrations in James B. Meriwether, *The Literary Career of William Faulkner*. Another copy of the booklet contains fifty-three pages of hand-lettering and nine pages of line drawings. Some of the play's motifs come from other Faulkner works of that time — among them "A Poplar" and "Study" in *The Mississippian* as well as preliminary versions of the poetry he would later publish as *The Marble Faun* — and from the works of other writers, including Verlaine and Amy Lowell, the motif of a well-groomed woman walking the formal paths of her garden presumably owing something to Miss Lowell's "Patterns." Despite great differences of intention and surface, this play introduces some elements which appear in at least two other prose works Faulkner wrote during the 'twenties: the story of Sir Galwyn in the unpublished allegorical booklet titled *Mayday* and Quentin Compson's section of *The Sound and the Fury*. Among the characters of this play, though it is much farther removed than *Mayday* from Quentin's monologue, are Pierrot, the Shade of Pierrot, Marietta, and the Spirit of Autumn, this last figure presenting the significance of mortality as do the man named Time in *Mayday* and Quentin's father in *The Sound and the Fury*. The suggestion that the troubled Pierrot may have drowned in a river looks ahead to the drownings which end the lives of both Sir Galwyn and Quentin Compson.

During his period at the University of Mississippi, and probably rather early in it, Faulkner, according to a friend, wrote a brief, untitled, one-act play which apparently survived in only one copy. It shows how Ruth, an emancipated girl of the prohibition era, ends her engagement to the more worldly Francis and becomes engaged to pusillanimous Jim, who, though giving in to Ruth on all counts, wins her because, according to her, he is so dominating. One interested in identifying unsigned, unpublished works by Faulkner might like to feel at least the slightest of similarities between the quiet opening remark of this play and the noisy opening sentence of Jason's monologue in *The Sound and the Fury* as well as between the action of this play and the central motif of one of Faulkner's unpublished, fire-damaged, signed poems; but nothing whatever in the wording and plot of the play proves that it is by Faulkner.

Before two months of the autumn semester of his second year had passed, Faulkner withdrew from enrollment in the University, on November 5, 1920, and never again registered as a student. But this by no means severed his connection with the University's publications. Five days after he abandoned formal schooling *The Mississippian* brought out the first of a series of his literary articles: a review of a volume of W. A. Percy's poetry in which Faulkner made the interesting remark that Percy " — like alas! how many of us — suffered the misfortune of having been born out of his time." The second in this series of articles discussed Conrad Aiken, whose poetry Faulkner respected and frequently quoted admiringly to his University of Mississippi friends, as he did the poetry of James Joyce, a volume of which he often carried about the campus.

In May, 1921, *The Mississippian,* which retained

Faulkner's name on its staff roll as one of the "Contributing Editors" despite his having resigned as a student, published his poem "Co-Education at Ole Miss." And at the end of that 1920-1921 academic year the *Ole Miss* annual, which also had retained Faulkner's name on its staff roll, as one of its art editors, published four of his drawings and his unsigned poem "Nocturne" with its decorative border, featuring it as a two-page spread which was impressive in spite of the reversal of the sequence of the plates — presumably a printers' error.

Faulkner left Oxford during this period, staying for a time in New York City. One of his friends there was the writer Stark Young, a native of Mississippi whom he had known at Oxford. Young did more than offer Faulkner a temporary base in this unsettled period following college; for, as he has helpfully written in a letter, he was able to introduce Faulkner to Elizabeth Prall, "in whose house I had a room, the room Bill shared for a time." Later Elizabeth Prall, by then the wife of Sherwood Anderson, was to introduce Faulkner to her husband in New Orleans to begin an association which Faulkner has since described as one he remembers with great pleasure.

But before his important sojourn in New Orleans, Faulkner resumed for three years his association with the University of Mississippi. The University newspaper for Friday, December 9, 1921, in its "Locals" column reported: "William Falkner, former Ole Miss student, who has been in New York City for some time studying art, has returned to the University to take the temporary postmastership at the University post office." And another article in the same issue, noting that the "examination for the position was held Saturday in Oxford" for Faulkner and two other contestants, wished "the best man success." Faulkner won the position, and by March, 1922, his recommendation to become permanent postmaster reached the United States Senate for confirmation, which it received.

The month after he began work in the University's post office, Faulkner began contributing again to *The Mississippian,* with a review of Edna St. Vincent Millay's *Aria da Capo,* on January 13, 1922, and an article praising Eugene O'Neill, on February 3, 1922, both of them initialed "W.F."

Though he had published his first piece of fiction, "Landing in Luck," almost as soon as he had enrolled as a student, Faulkner had published no other piece of fiction in the more than two years that had passed when on March 10, 1922, *The Mississippian* printed a prose sketch, "The Hill," which it credited merely to "W.F." The sketch is so closely related to a poem by Faulkner — the tenth in *A Green Bough* — that there is no problem about ascription; but for confirmation that he wrote this and the four other *Mississippian* pieces signed "W.F." I am indebted to a former member of the newspaper's staff. The week following the appearance of this sketch *The Mississippian* printed the first part of an article by Faulkner called "American Drama: Inhibitions," which it completed in the next week's issue. That spring the *Ole Miss* annual for 1922 contained, on the page of the French Club, its last drawing by Faulkner, ending an association which had begun five years before when the annual had published the drawing which is Faulkner's first publication this investigation has been able to discover.

But by this time Faulkner was, of course, not so much withdrawing his work from the University of Mississippi's amateur publications and their relatively small circle of readers as he was moving toward professional publication for the larger audience which now, forty years later, is world-wide. When the *Ole Miss* annual was printing this last of its drawings by Faulkner, the first of his seven contributions to the *Double Dealer* — the poem titled "Portrait" — appeared in the June, 1922, issue of that national "little magazine," which was published at New Orleans, where Faulkner was later to turn to fiction.

Though Faulkner had brought out his last University poem in the spring of 1921, his concern with poetry was to continue for some years: He dated a few unpublished poems during his New Orleans months in 1925 and had published four in the *Double Dealer* by the time he left New Orleans for Europe on July 7, 1925. Other unpublished poems are dated on that European trip. In 1926, the period immediately following his return, he dated more poems, from Pascagoula, Mississippi. After he had published major novels he still showed his concern with poetry by publishing during 1932 several poems in an issue of *Contempo* which featured his work, and by bringing out in 1932 and 1933 *This Earth* and *A Green Bough*, volumes which included revisions of poems he had written at the University of Mississippi.

In December, 1922, the University newspaper published its last essay by Faulkner, a review article centering on three novels by Joseph Hergesheimer. Interestingly — though probably it is only coincidence — the subjects of his previous pieces of literary criticism in *The Mississippian* had been either poetry or drama while he was devoting his time to writing poems and plays, but now as he moved a little closer in time to the novelist he was to become, this final *Mississippian* review was Faulkner's only contribution to that newspaper about an author of fiction.

Possibly Faulkner made one more contribution to *The Mississippian* after this review of Hergesheimer. At the start of the last year of his postmastership, on January 11, 1924, the paper carried a large, humorous "advertisement" for a Bluebird Insurance Company which was dedicated to the happiness of students because it would protect them in their college courses by insuring them "against professors and other failures." This advertisement and those which followed it purported to have been purchased by a company composed of three men: a student who had just returned from England where he had been at Oxford as a Rhodes Scholar; one of Faulkner's post office assistants, who later would become postmaster when Faulkner resigned; and Faulkner. Each was listed as a "president" of the company.

The published accounts of Faulkner's life which mention the Bluebird Insurance Company seem to have assumed without question that Faulkner invented and developed this joke. One cannot with assurance label that interpretation wrong, but there is the possibility that much

— or all? — of this series of advertisements originated in the office of *The Mississippian* and that Faulkner and, perhaps, the other two men were drafted as "presidents" without their consent or knowledge. Linking the three men together as founders of the company may have struck the newspaper's staff as funny: When the returned Rhodes Scholar, whom a *Mississippian* news article of just this time called "the famous and inimitable," gave a talk to the Latin Club of the University about life at Oxford, England, the reporter described the talk rather disrespectfully, saying it had revealed that at Oxford University "luncheon was served in one's room and one only had to take one's dinner, doncher know, with the jolly rabble" and that there one "— can you believe it? — lets afternoon tea interfere with a hotly contested cricket match." The post office assistant had appeared — pleasantly enough — in a series of *Mississippian* columns which made fun of campus figures and also, along with Faulkner and others of the post office force, in an illustrated half page of the humor section of the 1922 *Ole Miss* which named the post office the "Postgraduate Club" with *"Hours:* 11:20 to 12:20 every Wednesday," *"Motto:* Never put the mail up on time," and *"Aim:* Develop postmasters out of fifty students every year." Faulkner's name had appeared on the formal roll of the University's "Freshman Literary Class" in the 1919-1920 *Ole Miss* as "Falkner, Count William," and he had been listed by the humor section of the *Ole Miss* for 1923 as, "Hardest Worker — Count Falkner" in the list of "Superlative Election" results which named

WE INSURE YOU!

MAKE OLE MISS A WINTER RESORT!

Insure yourself against professors and other failures. Let your failures pay your way through college. If the professors don't appreciate your brains, the co-eds will your money. Laugh at pop-writtens—they mean less pop-written checks.

Girls, Think of Your Feet!

Our Foot-Ease Dancing Policy for ladies beats Blue-Jay in stopping that after-dance pain. Take out one of our famous policies and then write your A. & M. friends to come over.

Boys, Why Worry?

If sweetie stands you up, let us be the one to worry. Our Broken-Hearted Policy for young men will make you laugh when sheik makes a date with her!

There was once a man who went hunting. When he was a long ways from home it began to rain very, very hard. Seeing no other shelter, the man crawled into a hollow log and went to sleep. When he awoke the log had swollen so that he could not get out. The man felt that his last days had come. At once he began to realize he had wasted most of his life and had failed to take out that policy when the BLUEBIRD salesman called the day before. This made him feel so small that he crawled right out of the little end of the log. Moral: Let the BLUEBIRD help you out of tight places.

THE BLUEBIRD INSURANCE CO.

"We Take Anything"

JAMES BELL, JR., *President.*   WILLIAM FALKNER, *President*
LOUIS JIGGETTS, *President*
BELL-FALKNER-JIGGETTS, *Unlimited, Underwriters*

such other involuntary electoral victors as "Most Popular Professor" and "Biggest Grouch," and through the years he had appeared in the "Hayseed Letters" columns of *The Mississippian* in which the correspondence between an imaginary bumpkin at college and his father back on the farm at Possum Trot gave the authors of the column opportunities to make jokes about students and faculty. As one example, in a September 21, 1920, letter the son wrote home: "Wel here I am back again at the best schule in the world. Me and Blind Jim [an afflicted Negro about the campus whom the students sometimes adopted as a class officer or unofficial member of the University's administration], T. J. Tubb and Hannibal, Bill Falkner and Paul Rogers is all here now so school can comminct whenever it wants to." Though the "president" of the Bluebird Insurance Company who had been a Rhodes Scholar had also been one of the two authors of those "Hayseed Letters" with their burlesquing of students and faculty, and though the "president" who was an assistant at the post office was listed with the Rhodes Scholar among the "Contributors to This Issue" of *The Mississippian* which carried the first Bluebird advertisement, it seems doubtful that the remaining "president," William Faulkner, would strongly have favored publishing among the defenses of the Company in its advertisement of February 15 such an item as this: "It is a gross injustice to say that President Falkner has *permanently* retired in the Post Office. He merely takes temporary naps — during business hours." Faulkner, whose sense of humor has clearly demonstrated that it includes himself, may have taken part in this series of advertisements, which did not end until many months later with a full-page notice in the *Ole Miss* annual; but until firmer evidence appears either way, admirers of his fiction should be kindly allowed at least to assume that if Faulkner did voluntarily help work up these Bluebird notices he did not write the more flat-footed parts of them, did not favor stretching the joke over such a long time, and had nothing whatever to do with the news article in the February 15 *Mississippian* which announced that the next day the campus would start "The Bluebird Game," in which "some popular young man," secretly the Bluebird, would "carry a striped letter" to deliver "to the first coed" who happened to ask whether he was the Bluebird. "The fortunate young lady" would receive a ticket to the movies and a Bluebird insurance policy. The first game was to be "solely for the coeds. The next solely for the eds." "Isn't a ticket to the show worth asking the question? Try it. You'll find it fun. Play the Bluebird game."

Whatever Faulkner's relationship to the Bluebird Insurance Company hoax, he had many pleasures in these years in addition to his writing. He kept up his practice of taking long walks into the countryside, often covering twelve or fifteen miles with Phil Stone on a Sunday, and sometimes going off on foot for jaunts lasting several days. He and his friends enjoyed driving about in his open white car, which was named, at least by some of the friends, "Snowflake," and must have offered a pleasant, and notable, variation in a time still affected by Henry Ford's legendary order to give them any color they want just so it's black. Faulkner also played golf frequently at the University — so competently that near the time of his resignation as postmaster he took part in an exhibition match with two touring professionals, one from Wisconsin and one from Indiana, and turned in the best score. When the managers of the exhibition passed a hat in the audience to collect money for the players to divide among themselves, Faulkner elected to remain, in golf, an amateur.

Always an athlete, an outdoorsman, and a man effectively concerned for the welfare of the young, Faulkner served during part of this period as scoutmaster of the Oxford Boy Scout troop. Former members recall with pleasure and admiration that at meetings, on day-long outings, and during periods in camp, such as one in late August, 1924, at a small lake northwest of Oxford, William Faulkner created an unusually pleasant atmosphere, so that in the complete absence of nervous, shouted adult discipline, the boys maintained sense and order and had a fine time. One former youth of Oxford, now an important scholar, recalls the interest Faulkner was able to give a game in which the problem was to creep undetected through the woods toward a central player, a game Faulkner introduced and the boys of Oxford much enjoyed. Faulkner himself enjoyed this association and must have disliked having to end it, for he obviously was a first-rate scoutmaster.

As postmaster in these years, however, his performance apparently left something to be desired. He is said by friends to have accepted the job with the greatest reluc-

At Left, the United States Post Office, University, Mississippi, when Faulkner was its Postmaster

tance. And to readers of today there is something preposterous about the future author of *The Sound and the Fury* and *Go Down, Moses* making a living sorting other people's Christmas cards. By September 2, 1924, a U.S. Post Office inspector with headquarters in Corinth, Mississippi, had written Faulkner a letter detailing patrons' complaints about undelivered letters and packages, his reading a great deal instead of maintaining ardent attendance at the stamp window, and his having in the process of publication a book which some patrons claimed was written at the post office. The inspector has since recalled that Faulkner said he was "glad the Post Office sent someone who had a sense of humor and realized what a 'hell of a job' " it was. At the end of October, 1924, after almost three years at the post office, Faulkner resigned and the next day in a moving letter to a friend reported that it was pleasant to be completely free again to write and that he intended never again to be so trapped no matter what the consequences. A few weeks later, on December 26, 1924, when *The Marble Faun* had been published, Faulkner gave a copy to the Post Office inspector, inscribed to him as one "to whose friendship I owe extrication from a very unpleasant situation."

About mid-October Faulkner may have begun planning his departure from the post office, from the University, and from Mississippi. If so, his poem titled "Mississippi Hills: My Epitaph," which survives in manuscripts dated October 17, 1924, and was much revised later for the booklet published as *This Earth* and for *A Green*

Bough, has additional poignance. In mid-December, 1924, his first book, *The Marble Faun,* was published in Boston, a volume of poems dedicated to the poet's mother; with a preface dated *"September 23, 1924"* written by Phil Stone, who had been instrumental in arranging for its publication; and bearing at its end, as a date line for the composition of the poems, *"April, May, June, 1919."* Some of Stone's prefatory — and prophetic — comments about the poetry in *The Marble Faun* also apply to many of Faulkner's early poems which are being reprinted here:

They are the poems of youth. . . . They belong inevitably to that period of uncertainty and illusion. . . . They also have the defects of youth — youth's impatience, unsophistication and immaturity. They have youth's sheer joy . . . and youth's sudden, vague, unreasoned sadness over nothing at all. . . . I think these poems show promise. They have an unusual feeling for words and the music of words, a love of soft vowels, an instinct for color and rhythm, and — at times — a hint of coming muscularity of wrist . . . a man who has real talent will grow, will leave these things behind, will finally bring forth a flower that could have grown in no garden but his own.

Immediately after the publication of *The Marble Faun,* the New Orleans *Times-Picayune,* under the headline, "Author Goes to Europe," and under the date line, "University, Miss., Dec. 16," announced:

William Falkner, author of "The Marble Faun," which he recently received from his New York publisher, is preparing to leave the University of Mississippi campus for England and Italy, where he will spend the winter months in study.

Young Falkner is expecting also to complete a number of poems started in this country.

But when Faulkner reached New Orleans to take a ship he postponed the trip and settled in the city's French Quarter for several important months in which he changed from a writer who had expected to continue, as in his University years, to devote his energy to poetry into a writer who was to give his energy during the next decades to fiction — and with magnificent results. It was in New Orleans that Faulkner almost at once began writing sketches for the *Double Dealer* and for the *Picayune,* the first fiction for which he had received payment; and within a few months of his arrival at New Orleans he had completed *Soldiers' Pay,* the first of his many novels.

During his months in New Orleans Faulkner returned from time to time to the University of Mississippi, where, in addition to dating the manuscript of an unpublished poem from there on February 26, 1925, he took some part in the production of a University humor magazine called *The Scream,* being officially listed on the staff in 1925 as one of the art editors. Associates remember that he possibly made designs and drawings for another humor magazine, but whether he did or not remains uncertain and the drawings have not come to light. In May, 1925, a few weeks before he left New Orleans for Europe, *The Scream* printed three pieces of work which are the last this investigation has found signed by Faulkner in any University of Mississippi publication. Just as his first three signed contributions had been eight years before, these three were drawings.

But Faulkner's connection with *The Scream* was not quite over with their publication or even with the publication the next autumn of an unsigned drawing showing a man dangling outside an airplane in death drag acrobatics which seems to be in Faulkner's style. Not until May of 1927, when he had already published his second novel, did the staff of *The Scream,* financially pressed and appreciative of his draftsmanship, cut in half their 1925 plate of his drawing showing two men watching three women boarding a streetcar and print the parts as illustrations of two jokes, to end by a kind of amitosis the series of contributions to University of Mississippi publications which William Faulkner had begun in 1917.

CAMDEN FREE LIBRARY
EAST BRANCH

William Faulkner:

Early Prose and Poetry

WILLIAN
PALMER

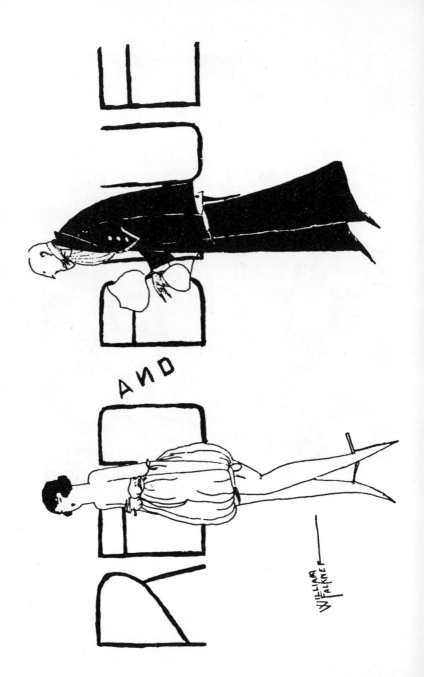

L'Apres-Midi d'un Faune

I follow through the singing trees
Her streaming clouded hair and face
And lascivious dreaming knees
Like gleaming water from some place
Of sleeping streams, or autumn leaves
Slow shed through still, love-wearied air.
She pauses: and as one who grieves
Shakes down her blown and vagrant hair
To veil her face, but not her eyes —
A hot quick spark, each sudden glance,
Or like the wild brown bee that flies
Sweet winged, a sharp extravagance
Of kisses on my limbs and neck.
She whirls and dances through the trees
That lift and sway like arms and fleck
Her with quick shadows, and the breeze
Lies on her short and circled breast.
Now hand in hand with her I go,
The green night in the silver west
Of virgin stars, pale row on row
Like ghostly hands, and ere she sleep
The dusk will take her by some stream
In silent meadows, dim and deep —
In dreams of stars and dreaming dream.

I have a nameless wish to go
To some far silent midnight noon

Where lonely streams whisper and flow
And sigh on sands blanched by the moon,
And blond limbed dancers whirling past,
The senile worn moon staring through
The sighing trees, until at last,
Their hair is powdered bright with dew.
And their sad slow limbs and brows
Are petals drifting on the breeze
Shed from the fingers of the boughs;
Then suddenly on all of these,
A sound like some great deep bell stroke
Falls, and they dance, unclad and cold —
It was the earth's great heart that broke
For springs before the world grew old.

WILLIAM FAULKNER.

CATHAY.

Sharp sands, those blind desert horsemen, sweep
Where yesterday tall shining carvels
Swam in thy golden past. What Fate foretells
That now the winds go lightly, lest thy sleep
Be broken? Where once thy splendors rose,
And cast their banners bright against the sky,
Now go the empty years infinitely
Rich with thy ghosts. So is it: who sows
The seed of Fame, makes the grain for Death to reap.

Wanderers, with faces sharp as spears,
And flocks and herds on aimless muffled feet
Drift where glittering kings went through each street
Of thy white vanished cities, and the years
Have closed like walls behind them. Still
Through the spawn of lesser destinies,
We stare, where once thy stars burned, lest like these,
We lose faith. They know thee not, nor will
To see thy magic empire when the Hand
Thrusts back the curtain of the shifting sand,
On singing stars and lifting golden hill.

William Falkner,
University Mississippi.

LANDING IN LUCK.

By William Falkner.

The machine levelled off and settled on the aerodrome. It turned and taxied back and stopped, headed into the wind again, its engine running idle. The instructor in the forward cockpit faced about and raised his goggles.

"Fairish," he said, "not so bad. How many hours have you had?"

Cadet Thompson, a "barracks ace," who had just made a fairly creditable landing, assumed an expression of assured confidence.

"Seven hours and nine minutes, sir."

"Think you can — hold that stick back, will you? — think you can take her round alone?"

"Yes, sir," he answered as he had answered at least four times a day for the last three days, with the small remaining part of his unconquered optimism in his voice. The instructor climbed slowly out onto the lower wing, then to the ground, stretching his legs. He got a cigarette from his clothes after a fashion resembling sleight-of-hand.

"You've got to solo some day. The C. O. gave us all a raggin' last night. It's chaps like you that give this stage such a name for inefficiency. Here you have had seven hours, and yet you never know if you are goin' to land on this aerodrome or down at Borden. And then you always pick a house or another machine to land on. What ever brought you to think you could fly? Swear I don't know what to do with you. Let you try it and break your neck, cr recommend you for discharge. Get rid of you either way, and a devilish good thing, too."

A silence hung heavily about Thompson's unhappy head. The instructor, sucking his cigarette, stared off across the aerodrome, where other wild and hardy amateurs took off, landed and crashed. A machine descended tail high, levelled off too soon and landed in a series of bumps like an inferior tennis ball.

"See that chap there? He's probably had half your time but he makes landings alone. But you, you cut your gun and sit up there like a blind idiot and when you condescend to dive the bus, you try your best to break our necks, yours and mine too; and I'll say right now, that's somethin' none of you rockin' chair aviators is goin' to do. Well, it's your neck or my reputation, now. Take her off, and what ever you do, keep your nose down."

Thompson pulled down his goggles. He had been angry enough to kill his officer for the better part of a week, so added indignities rested but lightly upon him. He was a strange mixture of fear and pride as he opened the throttle wide and pushed the stick forward — fear that he would wreck the machine landing, and pride that he was on his own at last. He was no physical coward, his fear was that he would show himself up before his less fortunate friends to whom he had talked largely of spins and side slips and gliding angles.

All-in-all, he was in no particularly safe frame of mind for his solo flight. He gained speed down the field. The tail was off the ground now and Thompson, more or less nervous, though he had taken the machine off like a veteran with the instructor aboard, pulled the stick back before the machine had gained speed sufficient to rise. It lurched forward and the tail sank heavily, losing more speed. He knew that he had gone too far down the field and should turn back and take off again, so he closed the throttle. When the noise of the engine ceased he heard the instructor shouting at him, and the splutter of a motor cycle. Sending after him, were they? Cadet Thompson was once more cleanly angry. He jerked the throttle open.

His subconscious mind had registered a cable across the end of the field, and he had flown enough to know that it was touch and go as to whether he would clear it. He was afraid of rising too soon again and he knew that he would not stop in time were he to close the throttle now. So, his eyes on the speed indicator, he pulled the stick back. The motion at once became easier and he climbed as much as he dared.

A shock; he closed his eyes, expecting to go over and down on his back in the road below. When nothing happened he ventured a frightened hurried glance. Below him was the yellow of a wheat field and the aerodrome far to the rear.

So the cable had broken! Must have, for here he was still going forward. His altimeter showed two hundred feet. Thompson felt like shouting. Now he'd show 'em what flying was. Rotten, was he? He'd pull a perfect landing and walk up to that officer and tell him just what kind of a poor fish he was.

"Blasted Englishman," he said, "thinks he's the only man in this wing who can really fly. Bet if he'd a' hit that cable he'd a' been on his back in that road, right now. Wish t'hell he was."

He made his turn carefully. Below at the edge of the aerodrome stood the ambulance, its crew gaping foolishly at him. "Like fish," he thought, "like poor fish." He leaned out of his cockpit and gestured pleasantly at them, a popular gesture known to all peoples of the civilized world.

Eight hundred feet. "High enough," he decided, and made another circle, losing height. He picked his spot on the field. "Now," he thought, cut the throttle and pushed the stick forward. He found a good gliding angle, wires singing, engine idle and long flames wrapping back from the exhausts. The field was filled with people running about and flapping their arms. Another machine rose to meet him. He opened the throttle and closed it again, a warning. "Why'n the hell don't they get off and lemme land?" he wondered.

The other machine passed him in a long bank, its occupants shouting at him; one of them carried something to which he gestured and pointed frantically. Thompson came out of his dive. They circled again and he saw that the object was about the size and shape of a wheel? A wheel from the landing gear of a machine. What kind of a joke was this? Why had they brought a wheel up to show him? He'd seen lots of wheels. Had two on his machine — on his machine — wheels? Then Thompson remembered the cable. He had stripped a wheel on that cable, then. There was nothing else it could mean. His brain assimilated this fact calmly. Having lost a wheel, he had nothing to land on. Therefore it were quite pointless to bother about landing, immediately, anyway. So he circled off and climbed, followed cautiously by the other machine, like two strange dogs meeting.

"Sir," said an orderly, entering the mess where the C. O. and three lesser lights were playing bridge, "sir, the Flight Commander, B Flight, reports that a cadet is abaht to crash."

" 'Crash?' " repeated the C. O.

"Out 'ere, sir. Yes, sir, 'e 'assn't got no landing gear."

" 'No landing gear?' What's this? What's this?"

"Yes, sir. 'E wiped it orf a-taking orf, sir. 'E's abaht out of petrol and the Flight Commander says 'e'll be a-coming down soon, sir."

"My word," said the C. O., going to the door and closely followed by the others.

"There 'e is, sir, that's 'im in front."

"My word," said the C. O. again and went off toward the hangars at a very good gait.

"What's this? What's this?" Approaching the group of officers.

"Cadet Thompson, sir," volunteered one, "Mr. Bessing's cadet. Oh, Bessing!"

Bessing came over, lifting his feet nervously.

"What's all this, Mr. Bessing?" The C. O. watched him narrowly. An instructor gets a bad name when his cadet crashes, he is responsible for the cadet's life as well as the machine.

"Rotten take off, sir. He tried to rise too soon, and when he failed, instead of comin' back and tryin' again, he carried right on. Struck that cable and lost his right wheel and he's been sittin' up there ever since. We sent another chap up to pull him up a bit. He's almost out of petrol and he'll have to come down soon."

"H-m. Didn't send him up too soon, did you, Mr. Bessing?"

"Chap's had seven hours, sir," he protested, and produced Thompson's card.

The C. O. studied it a moment, then returned it.

"Wharton, sir?" He helped the C. O. to a light and lit a cigarette for himself.

"Good lad, good lad," said the C. O., shading his eyes as he stared into the sky. "Something in you people at this wing, though. Cadets and officers both. N. C. O.'s got it, too. G. O. C. gave me a jolly raggin' not a fortnight ago. Do something. Do something, swear I will."

The drone from the engines above suddenly ceased. Thompson was out of petrol at last. The two machines descended in a wide spiral, and they on the earth stood watching him as he descended, as utterly beyond any human aid as though he were on another planet.

"Here they come," Bessing muttered half aloud. "If he only remembers to land on his left wing — the fool, oh, the blind, bounding fool!"

For Thompson's nerve was going as he neared the earth. The temptation was strong to kick his rudder over and close his eyes. The machine descended, barely retaining headway. He watched the approaching ground utterly unable to make any pretence of levelling off, paralyzed; his brain had ceased to function, he was all staring eyes watching the remorseless earth. He did not know his height, the ground rushed past too swiftly to judge, but he expected to crash any second. Thompson's fate was on the laps of the Gods.

The tail touched, bounded, scraped again. The left wing was low and the wing tip crumpled like paper. A tearing of fabric, a strut snapped, and he regained dominion over his limbs, but too late to do anything — were there anything to be done. The machine struck again, solidly, slewed around and stood on its nose.

Bessing was the first to reach him.

"Lord, Lord!" he was near weeping from nervous tension. "Are you all right? Never expected you'd come through, never expected it! Didn't think to see you alive! Don't ever let anyone else say you can't fly. Comin' out of that was a trick many an old flyer couldn't do! I say, are you all right?"

Hanging face downward from the cockpit, Cadet Thompson looked at Bessing, surprised at the words of this cold, short tempered officer. He forgot the days of tribulation and insult in this man's company, and his recent experience, and his eyes filled with utter adoration. Then he became violently ill.

That night Thompson sat gracefully on a table in the writing room of a down town hotel, tapping a boot with his stick and talking to sundry companions.

"— and so, when my petrol gave out, I knew it was up to me. I had already thought of a plan — I thought of several, but this one seemed the best — which was to put my tail down first and then drop my left wing, so the old bus wouldn't turn over and lie down on me. Well, it worked just as I had doped it out, only a ditch those fool A. M.'s had dug right across the field, mind you, tripped her up and she stood on her nose. I had thought of that, too, and pulled my belt up. Bessing said — he's a pretty good scout —"

"Ah-h-h —" they jeered him down profanely.

"Look at the nerve he's got, will you?"

"He'—"

"Ah, we know you! Why, the poor bum crashed on his solo, and listen at the line he's giving us!"

"Well, Bessing said —"

"Bessing said! Bessing said! Go tell the G.O.C. what Bessing said!"

"Dammit, don't I know what Bessing said? Ask him! That's all. You're a bunch of poor hams that think you can fly! Why, I got an hour and a half solo time. You poor fish. Ask Bessing! there's a guy that knows what's what."

He flung out of the room. They watched him with varying expressions.

"Say," spoke one, a cadet but recently enlisted and still in ground school: "D' you think he really did all that? He must be pretty good."

"That guy? That guy fly? He's so rotten they can't discharge him. Every time he goes up they have to get a gun and shoot him down. He's the 'f' out of flying. Biggest liar in the R.A.F."

Thompson passed through again, with Bessing, and his arm was through the officer's. He was deep in discussion evidently, but he looked up in time to give them a cheerfully condescending:

"Hello, you chaps."

SAPPHICS.

So it is: sleep comes not on my eyelids.
Nor in my eyes, with shaken hair and white
Aloof pale hands, and lips and breasts of iron,
   So she beholds me.

And yet though sleep comes not to me, there comes
A vision from the full smooth brow of sleep,
The white Aphrodite moving unbounded
   By her own hair.

In the purple beaks of the doves that draw her,
Beaks straight without desire, necks bent backward
Toward Lesbos and the flying feet of Loves
   Weeping behind her.

She looks not back, she looks not back to where
The nine crowned muses about Apollo
Stand like nine Corinthian columns singing
   In clear evening.

She sees not the Lesbians kissing mouth
To mouth across lute strings, drunken with singing,
Nor the white feet of the Oceanides
   Shining and unsandalled.

Before her go cryings and lamentations
Of barren women, a thunder of wings,
While ghosts of outcast Lethean women, lamenting,
　Stiffen the twilight.

William Falkner,
University, Miss.

AFTER FIFTY YEARS.

Her house is empty and her heart is old,
And filled with shades and echoes that deceive
No one save her, for still she tries to weave
With blind bent fingers, nets that cannot hold.
Once all men's arms rose up to her, 'tis told,
And hovered like white birds for her caress:
A crown she could have had to bind each tress
Of hair, and her sweet arms the Witches' Gold.

Her mirrors know her whiteness, for there
She rose in dreams from other dreams that lent
Her softness as she stood, crowned with soft hair.
And with his bound heart and his young eyes bent
And blind, he feels her presence like shed scent,
Holding him body and life within its snare.

W. FAULKNER.

UNE BALLADE DES FEMMES PERDUES

'Mais où sont les neiges d'antan'

I sing in the green dusk
Fatuously
Of ladies that I have loved
— Ça ne fait rien! Hélas, vraiment, vraiment

Gay little ghosts of loves in silver sandals
They dance with quick feet on my lute strings
With the abandon of boarding school virgins
While unbidden moths
Amorous of my white seraglio
Call them with soundless love songs
A sort of ethereal seduction

They hear, alas
My women
And brush my lips with little ghostly kisses
Stealing away
Singly, their tiny ardent faces
Like windflowers from some blown garden of dreams
To their love nights among the roses

I am old, and alone
And the star dust from their wings
Has dimmed my eyes
I sing in the green dusk
Of lost ladies — Si vraiment charmant, charmant.
— W. Falkner.

NAIADS' SONG.

Come ye sorrowful and keep
Tryst with us here in wedded sleep,
The silent noon lies over us
And shaken ripples cover us,
Our arms are soft as is the stream.
Come keep with us our slumbrous dream
Disheartened ones, if ye are sad,
If ye are in a garment clad
Of sorrow, come with us to sleep
In undulations dim and deep;
Where sunlight spreads and quivering lies
To draw in golden reveries
Its fingers through our glistered hair,
Finding profound contentment there.

Come ye sorrowful and weep
No more in waking, come and steep
Yourselves in us as does the bee
Plunge in the rose that, singing, he
Has opened. Here our mouths unfold
As does a flower bare its gold;
Our mouths are soft as any rose
That in a high walled garden grows,
A garden level as a cup
With the sunlight that fills it up.

Come ye sorrowful and sleep
Within our arms beneath the sweep
Of winds that whisper in the trees,
And boughs that whisper to the breeze
In a sad extravagance
Of dancers in a hushed dance;
When Pan sighs and his pipes doth blow
While sky above and earth below
Stand still and hearken to his strain,
And sigh also as does the rain
Through woodland lanes remote and cool
To dream upon a leafed pool.

Come ye sorrowful and keep
Tryst with us here in wedded sleep,
Our eyes are soft as twilit streams,
Our breasts are soft as silken dreams
And white at dusk; our breasts the beds
On which we soothe all aching heads,
Binding each in a scented tress
Till glides he in forgetfulness,
While the night sighs and whispers by
Sowing stars across the sky.
Come ye sorrowful and keep
Here in unmeasured dream and sleep.

— W. FALKNER.

FANTOCHES.

à Paul Verlaine.

Scaramouches and Pucinella
Cast one shadow on the mellow
Night, and kiss against the sky

And the doctor of Bogona
In his skull cap and kimono
Seeks for simples with pale avid eye

While his daughter half naked
Glides trembling from her narrow bed
To meet her lover waiting in the moon

Her lover from the Spanish Main
Whose passion thrills her with a strain
La lune ne garde aucune rancune

W. FALKNER.

CLAIR DE LUNE.

From PAUL VERLAINE.

Your soul is a lovely garden, and go
There masque and bergamasque charmingly,
Playing the lute and dancing and also
Sad beneath their disguising fanchise.*

All are singing in a minor key
Of conqueror love and life opportune,
Yet seem to doubt their joyous revelry
As their song melts in the light of the moon.

In the calm moonlight, so lovely fair
That makes the birds dream in the slender trees,
While fountains dream among the statues there;
Slim fountains sob in silver ecstasies.

— W. FALKNER.

* See Notes on the Text, page 128.

STREETS.

FROM PAUL VERLAINE.

Dance the Jig!

I loved her pretty eyes
Fairer than starry skies
And bright with malicious subtleties

Dance the Jig!

She had those dainty airs
That fill poor hearts with tears
Ah, how truly charming were her airs

Dance the Jig!

But this solace is mine
To kiss her mouth and find
That now to her my heart is deaf and blind

Dance the Jig!

Her face will ever be
In my mind's infinity
She broke the coin and gave it half to me

Dance the Jig!

— W. FALKNER.

[59]

A POPLAR.

Why do you shiver there
Between the white river and the road?
You are not cold,
With the sun light dreaming about you;
And yet you lift your pliant supplicating arms as though
To draw clouds from the sky to hide your slenderness.

You are a young girl
Trembling in the throes of ecstatic modesty,
A white objective girl
Whose clothing has been forcibly taken away from her.

— W. FALKNER.

A CLYMÈNE.

(From Paul Verlaine.)

Mystical chords
Songs without words
Dearest, because your eyes
Color of the skies.

Because your voice estranges
My vision, and deranges
And troubles the horizon
Of my reason.

Because your hidden slightness
Like a swan's graceful whiteness
Has filled my soul's room
With your perfume.

Because all of my being
In my breathing and seeing
Is a lingering like flowers
Of your hours.

A nimbus that dances
In my heart and entrances,
So shall it ever be
Through infinity.

W. FALKNER.

STUDY.

Somewhere a slender voiceless breeze will go
Unlinking the shivering poplars' arms, and brakes
With sleeves simply crossed where waters flow;
A sunless stream quiet and deep, that slakes
The thirsty alders pausing there at dawn.
(Hush, now, hush. Where was I? Jonson)

Somewhere a candle's guttering gold
Weaves a tapestry upon a cottage wall
And her gold hair, simple fold on fold,
While I can think of nothing else at all
Except the sunset in her eyes' still pool.
(Work, work, you fool! —)

Somewhere a blackbird lost within a wood
Whistles through its golden wired throat;
Some ways are white with birches in a hood
Of silver shaken by his mellow note,
Trembling gaspingly as though in fear;
Where the timid violet first appear.

(Muted dreams for them, for me
Bitter science. Exams are near
And my thoughts uncontrollably
Wander, and I cannot hear

The voice telling me that work I must,
For everything will be the same when I am dead
A thousand years. I wish I were a bust
All head.)

— W. FALKNER.

ALMA MATER.

All our eyes and hearts look up to thee,
For here all our voiceless dreams are spun
Between thy walls, quiet in dignity
Lent by the spirits of them whose lives begun
Within thy portals. Through them we can see
Upon the mountain top the shining sun
Success, drawing us infinitely
Upwardly, until Life and Task are one.

The beginning, not the end, is this.
Onward, by her unremitting grace
With memories that nothing can efface
Throned securely in our hearts; to kiss
— Holding, and held by her in fond embrace —
At parting, her kind calmly dreaming face.

— W. FALKNER.

CLASSES

Organizations

Le grand   Americaine   Parlez-vous Anglais, mam'zelle?
La petite Francaise — Mais oui, m'sieur, un   peu; Do you love me? keez me queek! Damn! 'ell!

SOCIAL ACTIVITIES

RED & BLUE

To a Co-ed

The dawn herself could not more beauty wear
Than you 'mid other women crowned in grace,
Nor have the sages known a fairer face
Than yours, gold-shadowed by your bright sweet hair.
Than you does Venus seem less heavenly fair;
The twilit hidden stillness of your eyes,
And throat, a singing bridge of still replies,
A slender bridge, yet all dreams hover there.

I could have turned unmoved from Helen's brow,
Who found no beauty in their Beatrice;
Their Thais seemed less lovely then as now,
Though some had bartered Athens for her kiss.
For down Time's arras, faint and fair and far,
Your face still beckons like a lonely star.

W. Falkner.

BOOKS AND THINGS

We are presenting this week a review by William S. [*sic*] Falkner of "In April Once" by W. A. Percy, Yale University Press; later we shall give a discussion of some of the poets who are representative of the spirit of the present in the form and content of their verse.

In April Once by W. A. Percy

Mr. Percy is a native Mississippian, a graduate of the University of the South and of the Harvard Law School. He was a member of the Belgian Relief Commission in the early days of the war, then served as a lieutenant attached to the 37th Division. He now lives in Greenville.

Mr. Percy — like alas! how many of us — suffered the misfortune of having been born out of his time. He should have lived in Victorian England and gone to Italy with Swinburne, for like Swinburne, he is a mixture of passionate adoration of beauty and as passionate a despair and disgust with its manifestations and accessories in the human race. His muse is Latin in type — poignant ecstasies of lyrical extravagance and a short lived artificial strength achieved at the cost of true strength in beauty.

Beauty, to him, is almost like physical pain, evident in the simplicity of this poem which is the nearest perfect thing in the book —

> I heard a bird at break of day
>> Sing from the autumn trees
> A song so mystical and calm,
>> So full of certainties,
> No man, I think, could listen long
>> Except upon his knees.
> Yet this was but a simple bird
>> Alone, among dead trees.

The influence of the frank pagan beauty worship of the past is heavily upon him, he is like a little boy closing his eyes against the dark of modernity which threatens the bright simplicity and the colorful romantic pageantry of the middle ages with which his eyes are full. One can imagine him best as a violinist who became blind about the time Mozart died, it would seem that the last thing he saw with his subjective intellect was Browning standing in naive admiration before his own mediocrity, of which Mr. Percy's "Epistle from Corinth" is the fruit. This is far and away the best thing in the book, and would have been better except for the fact that Mr. Percy, like every man who has ever lived, is the victim of his age.

As a whole, the book sustains its level of lyrical beauty. Occasionally it becomes pure vowelization, for it is not always the word that Mr. Percy seeks, but the sound. There is one element that will tend more than anything else to help it oblivionward, this is the section devoted to war poems. How many, many, many reams of paper that have been ruined with poetry appertaining to the late war no one, probably, will ever know, yet still the nightingales wear swords and Red Cross brassards.

Mr. Percy has not written a great book, — there is too much music in it for that, he is a violinist with an inferior instrument — yet (and most unusual as modern books of poetry go) the gold outweighs the dross. How much, I would not undertake to say, for he is a difficult person to whom to render justice; like Swinburne, he obscures the whole mental horizon, one either likes him passionately or one remains forever cold to him.

BOOKS & THINGS

Turns and Movies.

By Conrad Aiken. Houghton Mifflin Company.

In the fog generated by the mental puberty of contemporary American versifiers while writing inferior Keats or sobbing over the middle west, appears one rift of heaven sent blue — the poems of Conrad Aiken. He, alone of the entire yelping pack, seems to have a definite goal in mind. The others — there are perhaps half a dozen exceptions — are so many loud sounds lost in a single depth of privet hedge; the others lay about them lustily with mouth open and eyes closed, some in more or less impenetrable thickets of Browningesque obscurity, others hopelessly mired in the swamps of mediocrity, and all are creating a last flurry before darkness kindly engulfs them.

Many of them have realized that aesthetics is as much a science as chemistry, that there are certain definite scientific rules which, when properly applied, will produce great art as surely as certain chemical elements, combined in the proper proportions, will produce certain reactions; yet Mr. Aiken alone has made any effort to discover them and apply them intelligently. Nothing is ever accidental with him, he has most happily escaped our national curse of filling each and every space, religious, physical, mental and moral, and beside him the British nightingales, Mr. Vachel Lindsay with his tin pan and iron spoon, Mr. Kreymborg with his lithographic water coloring, and Mr. Carl Sandburg with his sentimental Chicago propaganda are so many puppets fumbling in windy darkness.

Mr. Aiken has a plastic mind, he uses variation, inversion, change of rhythm and such metrical tricks with skillful effect, and his clear impersonality will never permit him to write poor verse. He is never a press agent as are so many of his contemporaries. It is rather difficult to quote an example from him, as he has written with certain musical forms in mind, and any division of his work corresponding to the accepted dimensions of a poem is as a single chord to a fugue; yet the three quatrains from Discordants:

> Music I heard with you was more than music,
> And bread I broke with you was more than bread;
> Now that I am without you, all is desolate;
> All that was once so beautiful is dead.
>
> Your hands once touched this table and this silver,
> And I have seen your fingers hold this glass.
> These things do not remember you, belovèd, —
> And yet your touch upon them will not pass.
>
> For it was in my heart you moved among them,
> And blessed them with your hands and with your eyes;
> And in my heart they will remember always, —
> They knew you once, O beautiful and wise.

This is one of the most beautifully, impersonally sincere poems of all time.

The most interesting phase of Mr. Aiken's work is his experiments with an abstract three dimensional verse patterned on polyphonic music form: The Jig of Forslin and The House of Dust. This is interesting because of the utterly unlimited possibilities of it, he has the whole world before him; for as yet no one has made a successful attempt to synthesize musical reactions with abstract documentary reactions. Miss Amy Lowell tried a polyphonic prose which, in spite of the fact that she has created some delightful statuettes of perfectly blown glass, is merely a literary flatulency; and it has left her, reed in hand, staring in naive surprise at the air whence her bubbles have burst.

Mr. Aiken has never been haphazard, he has developed steadily, never for a moment at a loss, yet it is almost impossible to discover where his initial impulse came from. At times it seems that he is completing a cycle back to the Greeks, again there seem to be faint traces of the French symbolists, scattered through his poems are bits of soft sonority that Masefield might have formed; and so at last one returns to the starting point — from where did he come, and where is he going? It is interesting to watch, for — say in fifteen years — when the tide of aesthetic sterility which is slowly engulfing us has withdrawn, our first great poet will be left. Perhaps he is the man.

W. FALKNER.

CO-EDUCATION AT OLE MISS.

Ernest says, to Ernestine —
Thou art my little queen — O,
    Thou art the girl
    Of all the world
Who makes my heart beat mean — O;
    For night and day
    When thou art away,
Thy fair face fills my bean — O,
    An lov'st thou me
    As I love thee,
Let's off to Gretna Green — O.

W. FALKNER.

FISH, FLESH, FOWL

A.E.F. CLUB

THINK HOW MANY TIMES THIS BIRD'S
BEEN KISSED. HE GOT A CROIX
DE GUERRE, WITH PALMS.

MARIONETTES

NOCTURNE.

Colombine leans above the taper flame:
Colombine flings a rose.
She flings a severed hand at Pierrot's feet.

Behind, a perpindicular wall of stars,
Below, a gleam of snows.
Pierrot spins and whirls, Pierrot is fleet;
He whirls his hands like birds upon the moon.

Pierrot spins and whirls . . . .
His eyes are filled with facets of many worlds
Of silver and blue and green,
And he would hide his head, yet the keen
     blue darkness

Cuts his arms away from his face.

Listen! A violin
Freezes into a blade, so bright and thin
It pierces through his brain, into his heart,
And he is spitted by a pin of music on the dark.

Swift the wisps of motion blown across the moon;
Colombine flings a paper rose, —
Pierrot flits like a white moth on blue dark.

Black the taper, sharp their mouths in starlight,
The sky with icy rootless flowers gauntly glows.
They are stiffly frozen, bright and stark.

BOOKS & THINGS

Aria da Capo: a Play in One Act, by Edna St. Vincent Millay.

Something new enough to be outstanding in this age of mental puberty, this loud gesturing of the aesthetic messiahs of our emotional Valhalla who have one eye on the ball and the other on the grandstand. In newspaper parlance Miss Millay might be said to have scored a 'beat'; truly so in the sense that her contemporaries (those of them who will ever become aware that she has done something 'different') will each wonder to himself why he or she did not think of it first, which is very natural. Here is an idea so simple that it does give to wonder why under heaven no one has thought of it before. Its simplicity is doubtless the reason.

The play is a slight thing in itself; the surprising freshness of the idea of a pastoral tragedy enacted and concluded by interlopers against a conventional background of paper streamers and colored confetti in the midst of a thoroughly artificial Pierrot and Columbine suite alone makes it worth a second glance. Yet, this is an unjust statement; for about all modern playwrights and versifiers offer us is a sterile clashing of ideas innocent of imagination; a species of emotional shorthand. *Aria da Capo* possesses more than a clever idea skilfully carried out, yet it is difficult to put the hand on just what makes it go; there is no unusual depth of experience, either mental or physical, to be traced from it other than those characteristics acquired without conscious effort by every young writer, from the reading done during the period of his mental development, either from choice or compulsion. The language is good; the rhyme neither faltering through too close attention, nor careless from lack of it; the choice of words, with one exception — a speech of Pierrot's which I do not remember contains a word of inexcusable crudeness — is sound: and — heaven sent genius — the play is not too long; i.e., no padding, no mental sofa pillows to break the fall of the doomed and tiring mind. A lusty tenuous simplicity; the gods have given Miss Millay a strong wrist; and though an idea alone does not make or mar a piece of writing, it is something; and this one of hers will live even though Miss Amy Lowell intricately festoons it with broken glass, or Mr. Carl Sandburg sets it in the stock yards, to be acted, of a Saturday afternoon, by the Beef Butchers' Union.

W. F.

AMERICAN DRAMA: EUGENE O'NEILL.

Some one has said — a Frenchman, probably; they have said everything — that art is preeminently provincial: i.e., it comes directly from a certain age and a certain locality. This is a very profound statement; for Lear and Hamlet and All's Well could never have been written anywhere save in England during Elizabeth's reign (this is proved by the Hamlets that have come out of Denmark and Sweden, and the All's Well of French comedy) nor could Madame Bovary have been written in any place other than the Rhone valley in the nineteenth century; and just as Balzac is nineteenth century Paris. But there are exceptions to this, as there are to all rules holding a particle of truth; two modern ones being Conrad and Eugene O'Neill. These two men are anomalies, Joseph Conrad especially; this man has overturned all literary tradition in this point. It is too soon yet to be committed about O'Neill, though young as he is, he is already a quantity to make one wonder at the truth of the above assertion.

It is not especially difficult — after a man has written

and passed on — to trace the threads which were drawn together by him and put on paper in the form of his own work. It can be seen how Shakespeare ruthlessly took what he needed from his predecessors and contemporaries, leaving behind him a drama which the hand does not hold blood that can cap; the German playwrights have obviously and logically followed their destinies according to the Teutonic standards of thought down to the work of Hauptmann and Moeller; Synge is provincial, smacking of the soil from which he sprang as no other modern does (Synge is dead now); while the one man who is accomplishing anything in American drama is a contradiction to all concepts of art.

This may be because of the fact that America has no drama or literature worth the name, and hence no tradition. If this be the reason, one must perforce believe that the Fates have indeed played a scurvy trick upon him in casting into twentieth century America a man who might go to astounding lengths in a land possessing traditions. Facts about Conrad, however, who is even more of a contradiction than O'Neill, supply a basis for hoping that chance is not diabolical enough to perpetrate such a thing; and also show what an incalculable, indefinable quantity genius — horrible word — is.

The most unusual factor about O'Neill is that a modern American should write plays about the sea. We have had no salt water traditions for a hundred years. The English are the wanderers, while we essentially are not. Yet here is a man, son of a New York political "boss," raised in New York City and a student at Princeton, who writes of the sea. He has been, through accident, a sailor himself: he was shanghaied aboard a South American bound vessel and was forced to make a voyage as an able seaman from Rio to Liverpool in order to get home. He is not physically strong, having congenitally weak lungs, hence must lead a careful life as regards hardship and exposure; and yet his first writing phase was dominated by the sea.

And he has written good healthy plays, and — a strange thing — New York has realized his possibilities. "The Emperor Jones" played there, and "The Straw" and "Anna Christie" are playing in New York this winter. These last two are later plays, not of the sea, but the thing that makes them go is the same that made "Gold" and "Diff'rent" go, that made the "Emperor Jones" rise up and swagger in his egoism and cruelty, and die at last through his own hereditary fears: they all possess the same clarity and simplicity of plot and language. Nobody since "The Playboy" has gotten the force behind stage language that O'Neill has. The Emperor Jones' "who dat dare whistle in de Emperor's palace?" goes back to the "Playboy's" "the likes of which would make the mitred bishops themselves strain at the bars of paradise for to see the lady Helen walking in her golden shawl."

He is still developing; his later plays "The Straw" and "Anna Christie" betray a changing attitude toward his characters, a change from a detached observation of his people brought low by sheer circumstance, to a more personal regard for their joys and hopes, their sufferings and despairs. Perhaps in time he will make something of the wealth of natural dramatic material in this country, the greatest source being our language. A national literature cannot spring from folk lore — though heaven knows, such a forcing has been tried often enough — for America is too big and there are too many folk lores: Southern negroes, Spanish and French strains, the old west, for these always will remain colloquial; nor will it come through our slang, which also is likewise indigenous to restricted portions of the country. It can, however, come from the strength of imaginative idiom which is understandable by all who read English. Nowhere to-day, saving in parts of Ireland, is the English language spoken with the same earthy strength as it is in the United States; though we are, as a nation, still inarticulate.

W. F.

THE HILL

Before him and slightly above his head, the hill crest was clearly laid on the sky. Over it slid a sibilant invisibility of wind like a sheet of water, and it seemed to him that he might lift his feet from the road and swim upward and over the hill on this wind which filled his clothing, tightening his shirt across his chest, flapping his loose jacket and trousers about him, and which stirred the thick uncombed hair above his stubby quiet face. His long shadow legs rose perpendicularly and fell, ludicrously, as though without power of progression, as though his body had been mesmerized by a whimsical God to a futile puppet-like activity upon one spot, while time and life terrifically passed him and left him behind. At last his shadow reached the crest and fell headlong over it.

The opposite valley rim came first into sight, azure and aloof, in the level afternoon sun. Against it, like figures rising in a dream, a white church spire rose, then house-tops, red and faded green and olive half hidden in budded oaks and elms. Three poplars twinkled their leaves against a gray sunned wall over which leaned peach and apple trees in an extravagance of fragile pink and white; and though there was no wind in the valley, bent narrowly to the quiet resistless compulsion of April in their branches, then were still and straight again except for the silver mist of their never ceasing, never escaping leaves. The entire valley stretched beneath him, and his shadow, springing far out, lay across it, quiet and enormous. Here and there a thread of smoke balanced precariously upon a chimney. The hamlet slept, wrapped in peace and quiet beneath the evening sun, as it had slept for a century; waiting, invisibly honeycombed with joys and sorrows, hopes and despairs, for the end of time.

From the hilltop the valley was a motionless mosaic of tree and house; from the hilltop were to be seen no cluttered barren lots sodden with spring rain and churned and torn by hoof of horse and cattle, no piles of winter ashes and rusting tin cans, no dingy hoardings covered with the tattered insanities of posted salacities and advertisements. There was no suggestion of striving, of whipped vanities, of ambition and lusts, of the drying spittle of religious controversy; he could not see that the sonorous simplicity of the court house columns was discolored and stained with casual tobacco. In the valley there was no movement save the thin spiraling of smoke and the heart-tightening grace of the poplars, no sound save the measured faint reverberation of an anvil.

The slow featureless mediocrity of his face twisted to an internal impulse: the terrific groping of his mind. His monstrous shadow lay like a portent upon the church, and for a moment he had almost grasped something alien to him, but it eluded him; and being unaware that there was anything which had tried to break down the barriers of his mind and communicate with him, he was unaware that he had been eluded. Behind him was a day of harsh labor with his hands, a strife against the forces of nature to gain bread and clothing and a place to sleep, a victory gotten at the price of bodily tissues and the numbered days of his existence; before him lay the hamlet which was home to him, the tieless casual; and beyond it lay waiting another day of toil to gain bread and clothing and a place to sleep. In this way he worked out the devastating unimportance of his destiny, with a mind heretofore untroubled by moral quibbles and principles, shaken at last by the faint resistless force of spring in a valley at sunset.

The sun plunged silently into the liquid green of the west and the valley was abruptly in shadow. And as the sun released him, who lived and labored in the sun, his mind that troubled him for the first time, became quieted. Here, in the dusk, nymphs and fauns might riot to a shrilling of thin pipes, to a shivering and hissing of cymbals in a sharp volcanic abasement beneath a tall icy star. * * * Behind him was the motionless conflagration of sunset, before him was the opposite valley rim upon the changing sky. For a while he stood on one horizon and stared across at the other, far above a world of endless toil and troubled slumber; untouched, untouchable; forgetting, for a space, that he must return. * * * He slowly descended the hill.

W. F.

BOOKS & THINGS

American Drama
Inhibitions

— 1 —

Only by means of some astounding blind machination
of chance will the next twenty-five years see in America
a fundamentally sound play — a structure solidly built,
properly produced and correctly acted. Playwrights and
actors are now at the mercy of circumstances which must
inevitably drive all imaginative people whose judgment
is not temporarily aberrant, to various conditions of
fancied relief; to a frank pandering to Frank Crane's
market — holding a spiritual spittoon, so to speak, for
that stratum which, unfortunately, has money in this
country — to Europe; and to synthetic whiskey.

Writing people are all so pathetically torn between a
desire to make a figure in the world and a morbid interest in their personal egos — the deadly fruit of the
grafting of Sigmund Freud upon the dynamic chaos of
a hodge-podge of nationalities. And, with characteristic
national restlessness, those with imagination and some
talent find it unbearable. O'Neill has turned his back on
America to write of the sea, Marsden Hartley explodes

vindicative fire crackers in Montmartre, Alfred Kreymborg has gone to Italy, and Ezra Pound furiously toys with spurious bronze in London. All have found America aesthetically impossible; yet, being of America, will some day return, a few into dyspeptic exile, others to write joyously for the movies.

— 2 —

We have, in America, an inexhaustible fund of dramatic material. Two sources occur to any one: the old Mississippi river days, and the romantic growth of railroads. And yet, when the Mississippi is mentioned, Mark Twain alone comes to mind: a hack writer who would not have been considered fourth rate in Europe, who tricked out a few of the old proven "sure fire" literary skeletons with sufficient local color to intrigue the superficial and the lazy.*

Sound art, however, does not depend on the quality or quantity of available material: a man with real ability finds sufficient what he has to hand. Material does aid that person who does not possess quite enough driving force to create living figures out of his own brain; wealth of material does enable him to build better than he otherwise could. No one in America — no writer — can detach himself from the national literary shibboleths and pogroms to do this, though; those who are doing worth while things really labor infinitely more than the results achieved would show, for the reason that they must over-

* Faulkner's opinion of Twain subsequently rose, until in recent years he has called *The Adventures of Huckleberry Finn* a candidate, with *Moby-Dick,* for consideration as the greatest American book. — C.C.

come all this self torture, must first slay the dragons which they, themselves, have raised. An apt instance was related to me by a dramatic critic on a New York magazine: Robert Edmund Jones, a designer of stage settings, discovered that, for some time, he had been subject to an intangible ailment. He found that the quality of his work had been mysteriously deteriorating, that his sleep and appetite were being undermined. A friend — perhaps the one who assisted him in discovering his alarming condition — advised him to repair to a certain practitioner of the new therapeutic psycho-analysis. He did so, was "siked," and immediately recovered his appetite, his untroubled slumber, and his old zest in stage designing. This is what all writers who are exposed to the prevailing literary tendencies in America must combat; and, so long as socialism, psycho-analysis and the aesthetic attitude are profitable as well as popular, so long will such conditions obtain.

One rainbow we have on our dramatic horizon: language as it is spoken in America. In comparison with it, British is a Sunday night affair of bread and milk — melodious but slightly tiresome nightingales in a formal clipped hedge. Other tongues are not considered here: the Northman is essentially the poet and playwright, as the Frenchman is the painter, and the German the musician. It does not always follow that a play built according to sound rules — i.e. simplicity and strength of language, thorough knowledge of material, and clarity of plot — will be a good play as a result; else playwriting would become a comparatively simple process. (Language means nothing to Shaw: except for the accident of birth he might well have written in French.) In America, however, with our paucity of mental balance, language is our logical savior. Very few authors are able to say anything simply; these extremists fluctuate between the manners of various dead-and-gone stylists — achieving therefrom a vehicle which might well serve to advertise soap and cigarettes — and sheer idiocy. Those who realize that language is our best bet employ slang and our "hard" colloquialisms in order to erect an edifice which resembles that of a mason who endeavors to build a skyscraper with brick alone, forgetting the need of a steel skeleton within it.

Our wealth of language and our inarticulateness (inability to derive any benefit from the language) are due to the same cause: our racial chaos and our instinctive quickness to realize our simpler needs, and to supply them from any source. As a nation, we are a people of action (the astounding growth of the moving picture industry is a proof); even our language is action rather than communication between minds: those who might be justly called men of ideas take their thinking consciously, a matter of mental agility like an inverted Swedish exercise, and they frankly and naively call upon all near them to see and admire.

This is the Hydra which we have raised, and which we become pessimists or idiots slaying; who have the fundamentals of the lustiest language of modern times; a language that seems, to the newly arrived foreigner, a mass of subtleties for the reason that it is employed only as a means of relief, when physical action is impossible or unpleasant, by all classes, ranging from the Harvard professor, through the gardeniaed aloof young liberal, to the lowliest pop vendor at the ball park.

W. F.

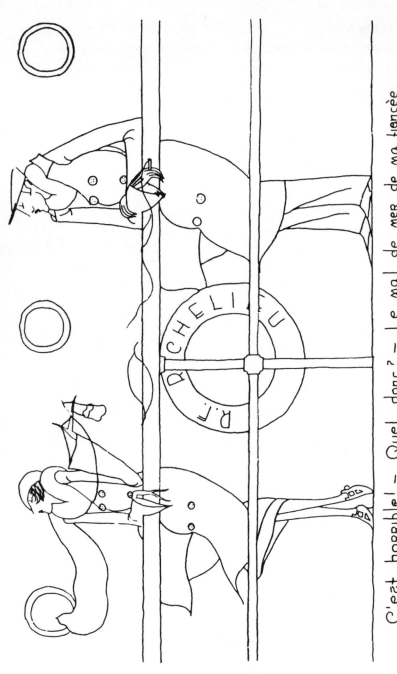

C'est horrible! – Quel donc? – Le mal de mer de ma fiancée.
La, pourquoi ne trouvez-vous pas une amie qui est orpheline?

Portrait

By WILLIAM FAULKNER

Raise your hand between us, to your face,
And draw the opaque curtains on your eyes.
Let us walk here, softly checked with shadow,
And talk of careful trivialities.

Let us lightly speak at random; tonight's movie,
Repeat a broken conversation, word for word;
Of friends, and happiness. The darkness scurries,
And we hear again a music both have heard

Singing blood to blood between our palms.
Come, lift your eyes, your tiny scrap of mouth
So lightly mobile on your dim white face;
Aloofly talk of life, profound in youth

And simple also. Young and white and strange
You walk beside me down this shadowed street,
Against my hand your small breast softly lies,
And your laughter breaks the rhythm of our feet.

You are so young. And frankly you believe
This world, this darkened street, this shadowed wall
Are dim with beauty you passionately know
Cannot fade nor cool nor die at all.

Raise your hand, then, to your scarce seen face,
And draw the opaque curtains on your eyes;
Profoundly speak of life, of simple truths,
The while your voice is clear with frank surprise.

BOOKS AND THINGS

JOSEPH HERGESHEIMER.

Linda Condon—Cytherea—The Bright Shawl.

No one since Poe has allowed himself to be enslaved by words as has Hergesheimer. What was, in Poe, however, a morbid but masculine emotional curiosity has degenerated with the age to a deliberate pandering to the emotions in Hergesheimer, like an attenuation of violins. A strange case of sex crucifixion turned backward upon itself: Mirandola and Cardinal Bembo become gestures in tinsel. He is subjective enough to bear life with fair equanimity, but he is afraid of living, of man in his sorry clay braving chance and circumstance.

He has never written a novel — someone has yet to coin the word for each unit of his work — Linda Condon, in which he reached his apex, is not a novel. It is more like a lovely Byzantine frieze: a few unforgettable figures in silent arrested motion, forever beyond the reach of time and troubling the heart like music. His people are never actuated from within; they do not create life about them; they are like puppets assuming graceful but meaningless postures in answer to the author's compulsions, and holding these attitudes until he arranges their limbs again in other gestures as graceful and as meaningless. His tact, though, is delicate and flawless — always a social grace. One can imagine Hergesheimer submerging himself in Linda Condon as in a still harbor where the age cannot hurt him and where rumor of the world reaches him only as a far faint sound of rain. Perhaps he wrote the book for this reason: surely a man of his delicacy and perception would never suffer the delusion that Linda Condon is a novel.

For this reason the book troubles the heart, the faintest shadow of an insistence; as though one were waked from a dream, for a space into a quiet region of light and shadow, soundless and beyond despair. La figlia della sua mente, l'amorosa l'idea.

Cytherea is nothing — the apostle James making an obscene gesture. Rather, the apostle James trying to carry off a top hat and a morning coat. A palpable and bootless attempt to ape the literary colors of the day.

The Bright Shawl is better. The sublimated dime novel peopled, like Cytherea, with morbid men and obscene women. But skilful; the tricks of the trade were never employed with better effect, unless by Conrad. The induction to The Bright Shawl is good — he talks of the shawl for a page or so before one is aware of the presence of the shawl as a material object, before the word itself is said; it is like being in a room full of people, one of whom one has not yet directly looked at, though conscious all the time of his presence.

These two books have swung to the opposite extreme

from Linda Condon. Hergesheimer has tried to enter life, with disastrous results; Sinclair Lewis and the New York Times have corrupted him. He should never try to write about people at all; he should spend his time, if he must write, describing trees or marble fountains, houses or cities. Here his ability to write flawless prose would not be tortured by his unfortunate reactions to the apish imbecilities of the human race. As it is, he is like an emasculate priest surrounded by the puppets he has carved and clothed and painted — a terrific world without motion or meaning.

W. F.

Appendix

On Criticism

By WILLIAM FAULKNER

WALT WHITMAN said, among bombast and muscle-bound platitudes, that to have great poets there must be great audiences too. If Walt Whitman realized this it should be universally obvious in this day of radio to inform us and the so-called high-brow magazines to correct our information; not to speak of the personal touch of the lecture platform. And yet, what have the periodicals and lecturers done to create either great audiences or great writers of us? Do these Sybils take the neophyte gently in hand and instruct him in the fundamentals of taste? They do not even try to inculcate in him a reverence for their mysteries, (thus robbing criticism of even its emotional value — and how else are you to control the herd, except through its emotions? Was there ever a logical mob?). Thus there is no tradition, no esprit de corps: All that is necessary for admission to the ranks of criticism is a typewriter.

They do not even try to mould his opinions for him. True, it is scarcely worth while moulding anyone's opinions for him, but it is pleasant pastime changing his opinion from one fallacy to another, for his soul's sake. The American critic, like the prestidigitator, tries to find just how much he can let the spectator see, and still get away with it — the superiority of the hand over the eye. He takes the piece under examination for an instrument upon which to run difficult arpeggios of cleverness. This seems so sophomoric, so useless; like the cornetist performing aural acrobatics while waiting for the band to assemble. With this difference: the cornetist gets tired after a while, and stops. The amazing possibility here occurs that the critic enjoys his own music. Do they, then enjoy reading each other? One can as easily imagine barbers shaving each other for fun.

The American critic blinds, not only his audience but himself as well, to the prime essential. His trade becomes mental gymnastics: he becomes a reincarnation of the side-show spell-binder of happy memory, holding the yokelry enravished, not with what he says, but how he says it. Their minds fly shut before the eye-filling meretricity of pyrotechnics. Who has not heard this conversation?

"Have you seen the last . . . (suit yourself)? Jones Brown is good this time; he . . . uh, What is that book? a novel, I think . . . on the end of my tongue . . . by some fellow. Anyway, Jones refers to him as an aesthetic boy scout. It's good: you must read it."

"Yes, I will: Brown is always good, do you remember what he said about someone: 'A parrot that couldn't fly and had never learned to curse'?"

And yet, when you ask him the author's name, or the

book's, or what it is about, he cannot tell you! He either has not read it, or has not only been unmoved by it but has waited to read Brown to form an opinion. And Brown has offered no opinion whatever. Perhaps Brown himself has none.

How much better they do this sort of thing in England than in America! Of course there are in America critics as sane and tolerant and as soundly equipped, but with a few exceptions they have no status: the magazines which set the standard ignore them; or finding conditions unbearable, they ignore the magazines and live abroad. In a recent number of "The Saturday Review" Mr. Gerald Gould, reviewing "The Hidden Player" by Alfred Noyes, says:

"People do not talk like that . . . It will not do to set down ordinary speech of ordinary people; that would generally be dull . . . To give the deadly detail is misleading." Here is the essential of criticism. So just and clear and complete: there is nothing more to be said. A criticism which not only the public, but the author as well, may read with profit. But what American critic would let it go at this? Who among our literary arbiters could miss this chance of referring to Mr. Noyes as "an aesthetic boy scout," or something else as sophomoric and irrelevant? And what reader could then pick up the book with an unbiased mind, without a faint unease of patronage and pity . . . not for the book, but for Mr. Noyes? One in a hundred. And what writer, with his own compulsions to suffer, with his own urge to disfigure paper harrying him like a gad-fly, could get any profit or nourishment from being referred to as an aesthetic boy scout? Not one.

Saneness, that is the word. Live and let live; criticise with taste for a criterion, and not tongue. The English review criticises the book, the American the author. The American critic foists upon the reading public a distorted buffoon within whose shadow the titles of sundry uncut volumes vaguely lurk. Surely, if there are two professions in which there should be no professional jealousy, they are prostitution and literature.

As it is, competition becomes cutthroat. The writer cannot begin to compete with the critic, he is too busy writing and also he is organically unfitted for the contest. And if he had time and were properly armed, it would be unfair. The critic, once he becomes a habit with his readers, is considered infallible by them; and his contact with them is direct enough to allow him always the last word. And with the American the last word carries weight, is culminative. Probably because it gives him a chance to talk some himself.

Dying Gladiator

By WILLIAM FAULKNER

What sorrow, love, that the wind and the raining wake?
Man's life is but an April without a morrow
Between a snow and a season of snow. What sorrow
That winter again about his head must break?

Man's life is short, nor lingers. Gods!
What April knew thee, Caia, in thy young whiteness!
The shepherd lad of thee had a new lightness
To magic him, a clod among other clods.

This was youth, the world a star and a hill:
Rome but an echo, untroubled of us, the immortals;
Torches were less, and trumpets aloft in the portals
Ringing his blood to a flame, that it might spill.

What sorrow, love? Bronze in an age of bronze
And life is but the gesture of a caesar,
Death the mistress that dying, alone, could please her,
Dying, he may force her bastions.

Briefer, love, briefer than all the pain
Of April and youth, are garland and leaf and swallow.
What sorrow, love, that a field for a space lay fallow?
What sorrow, love, for drouth, after the rain?

[*113*]

Verse Old and Nascent:

A Pilgrimage

By WILLIAM FAULKNER

AT THE age of sixteen, I discovered Swinburne. Or rather, Swinburne discovered me, springing from some tortured undergrowth of my adolescence, like a highwayman, making me his slave. My mental life at that period was so completely and smoothly veneered with surface insincerity — obviously necessary to me at that time, to support intact my personal integrity — that I can not tell to this day exactly to what depth he stirred me, just how deeply the footprints of his passage are left in my mind. It seems to me now that I found him nothing but a flexible vessel into which I might put my own vague emotional shapes without breaking them. It was years later that I found in him much more than bright and bitter sound, more than a satisfying tinsel of blood and death and gold and the inevitable sea. True, I dipped into Shelley and Keats — who doesn't, at that age? — but they did not move me.

I do not think it was assurance so much, merely complacence and a youthful morbidity, which counteracted them and left me cold. I was not interested in verse for verse's sake then. I read and employed verse, firstly, for the purpose of furthering various philanderings in which I was engaged, secondly, to complete a youthful gesture I was then making, of being "different" in a small town. Later, my concupiscence waning, I turned inevitably to verse, finding therein an emotional counterpart far more satisfactory for two reasons: (1) No partner was required (2) It was so much simpler just to close a book, and take a walk. I do not mean by this that I ever found anything sexual in Swinburne: there is no sex in Swinburne. The mathematician, surely; and eroticism just as there is eroticism in form and color and movement wherever found. But not that tortured sex in — say — D. H. Lawrence.

It is a time-honored custom to read Omar to one's mistress as an accompaniment to consummation — a sort of stringed obligato among the sighs. I found that verse could be employed not only to temporarily blind the spirit to the ungraceful posturings of the flesh, but also to speed onward the whole affair. Ah, women, with their hungry snatching little souls! With a man it is — quite often — art for art's sake; with a woman it is always art for the artist's sake.

Whatever it was that I found in Swinburne, it completely satisfied me and filled my inner life. I cannot understand now how I could have regarded the others with such dull complacency. Surely, if one be moved at all by Swinburne he must inevitably find in Swinburne's forerunners some kinship. Perhaps it is that Swinburne, having taken his heritage and elaborated it to the despair of any would-be poet, has coarsened it to tickle the dullest of palates as well as the most discriminating, as used water can be drunk by both hogs and gods.

Therefore, I believe I came as near as possible to approaching poetry with an unprejudiced mind. I was subject to the usual proselyting of an older person, but the strings were pulled so casually as scarcely to influence my point of view. I had no opinions at that time, the opinions I later formed were all factitious and were discarded. I approached Poetry unawed, as if to say; "Now, let's see what you have." Having used verse, I would now allow verse to use me if it could.

When the co-ordinated chaos of the war was replaced by the unco-ordinated chaos of peace I took seriously to reading verse. With no background whatever I joined the pack belling loudly after contemporary poets. I could not always tell what it was all about but "This is the stuff," I told myself, believing, like so many, that if one cried loudly enough to be heard above the din, and so convinced others that one was "in the know," one would be automatically accoladed. I joined an emotional B.P.O.E.

The beauty — spiritual and physical — of the South lies in the fact that God has done so much for it and man so little. I have this for which to thank whatever gods may be: that having fixed my roots in this soil all contact, saving by the printed word, with contemporary poets is impossible.

That page is closed to me forever. I read Robinson

and Frost with pleasure, and Aldington; Conrad Aiken's minor music still echoes in my heart; but beyond these, that period might have never been. I no longer try to read the others at all.

It was "The Shropshire Lad" which closed the period. I found a paperbound copy in a bookshop and when I opened it I discovered there the secret after which the moderns course howling like curs on a cold trail in a dark wood, giving off, it is true, an occasional note clear with beauty, but curs just the same. Here was reason for being born into a fantastic world: discovering the splendor of fortitude, the beauty of being of the soil like a tree about which fools might howl and which winds of disillusion and death and despair might strip, leaving it bleak, without bitterness; beautiful in sadness.

From this point the road is obvious, Shakespeare I read, and Spenser, and the Elizabethans, and Shelley and Keats. I read "Thou still unravished bride of quietness" and found a still water withal strong and potent, quiet with its own strength, and satisfying as bread. That beautiful awareness, so sure of its own power that it is not necessary to create the illusion of force by frenzy and motion. Take the odes to a nightingale, to a Grecian urn, "Music to hear," etc.; here is the spiritual beauty which the moderns strive vainly for with trickery, and yet beneath it one knows are entrails; masculinity.

Occasionally I see modern verse in magazines. In four years I have found but one cause of interest; a tendency among them to revert to formal rhymes and conventional forms again. Have they, too, seen the writing on the wall?

Can one still hope? Or is this age, this decade, impossible for the creation of poetry? Is there nowhere among us a Keats in embryo, someone who will tune his lute to the beauty of the world? Life is not different from what it was when Shelley drove like a swallow southward from the unbearable English winter; living may be different, but not life. Time changes us, but Time's self does not change. Here is the same air, the same sunlight in which Shelley dreamed of golden men and women immortal in a silver world and in which young John Keats wrote "Endymion" trying to gain enough silver to marry Fannie Brawne and set up an apothecary's shop. Is not there among us someone who can write something beautiful and passionate and sad instead of saddening?

The Faun

To H.L.

By WILLIAM FAULKNER

When laggard March, a faun whose stampings ring
And ripple the leaves with hiding: vain pursuit
Of May's anticipated dryad, mute
And yet unwombed of the moist flanks of spring;

Within the green dilemma of faint leaves
His panting puzzled heart is wrung and blind:
To run the singing corridors of wind,
Out-pace waned moons to May hand shapes and grieves;

Or, leafed close and passionate, to remain
And taste his bitter thumbs 'till May again
Left bare by wild vines' slipping, does incite
To strip the musiced leaves upon her breast
And from a cup unlipped, undreamt, unguessed,
Sip that wine sweet-sunned for Jove's delight.

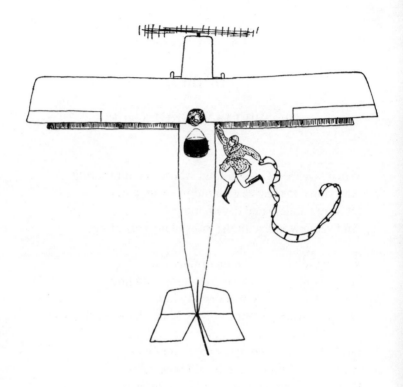

Notes on the Text

Notes on the Text

IN THE following notes William Faulkner's drawings, poems, and prose pieces which this volume reprints are listed in the order of their first published appearance — and therefore in the order of their appearance in this volume as well. When this reprinting has altered the original texts the alterations have been noted here.

Drawing of woman and bald man dancing: *Ole Miss,* 1916-1917, Vol. XXI, p. 163, introducing a section of "Social Activities."

Drawing of two men and a woman standing before a checkerboard background: *Ole Miss,* 1917-1918, Vol. XXII, p. 111, introducing a section of "Social Activities."

Drawing of woman and man standing before a background lettered "Red and Blue": *Ole Miss,* 1917-1918, Vol. XXII, p. 113, a page listing members of the Red and Blue Club, a dancing society.

"L'Apres-Midi d'un Faune": *The New Republic,* Vol. XX (August 6, 1919), p. 24. Later, in the University of Mississippi newspaper, *The Mississippian,* on October 29, 1919, page 4, Faulkner published the following, somewhat different, version of this poem, reproduced here verbatim:

L'Apres-Midi D'un Faune

I follow through the singing trees
Her streaming clouded hair and face
And lascivious dreaming knees
Like gleaming water from some place
Of sleeping streams, or autumn leaves
Slow shed through still love wearied air.
She pauses; and as one who grieves,
Shakes down her blown and vagrant hair
To veil her face, but not her eyes —
A hot quick spark, each sudden glance,
Or as the wild brown bee that flies
Sweet winged, a sharp extravagance
Of kisses on my limbs and neck.
She whirls and dances through the trees
That lift and sway like arms and fleck
Her with quick shadows, and the breeze
Lies on her short and circled breast.
Now hand in hand with her I go.
The green night in the silver west
Of virgin stars, pale row on row
Like ghostly hands, and ere she sleep
The dusk will take her by some stream
In silent meadows, dim and deep —
In dreams of stars and dreaming dream.

I have a sudden wish to go
To some far silent midnight moon,
Where lonely streams whisper and flow
And sigh on sands blanched by the moon.
And blond limbed dancers whirling past
The senile worn moon staring through
The sighing trees, until at last
Their hair is powdered bright with dew.
And their sad slow limbs and brows
Are petals drifting with the breeze,
Shed from the fingers of the boughs;
Then suddenly, on all of these
A sound, like some great deep bell stroke

Falls, and they dance, unclad and cold —
It was the earth's great heart that broke
For spring broke before the world grew old.

William Faulkner of University
of Mississippi. From the New
Republic, Aug. 6, 1919.

"CATHAY.": *The Mississippian*, November 12, 1919, p. 8. This poem was especially badly set in *The Mississippian*. Part of the emendation here derives not only from an attempt to estimate what alterations are logical but from examination of the three other versions of the poem mentioned in the introduction to this volume.

Line 1: *The Mississippian* printed only the first of the two commas in this line.

Line 3: "foretells" appeared in *The Mississippian* as "fortells."

Line 6: *The Mississippian* ended this line with a semicolon.

Line 14: *The Mississippian* indented this line.

Line 15: "spawn" appeared in *The Mississippian* as "span."

Line 17: *The Mississippian* printed "thee" as "the" and made "nor will" into a two-word succeeding line.

"LANDING IN LUCK.": *The Mississippian*, November 26, 1919, pp. 2 and 7. This story appeared in a column headed "WEEKLY SHORT STORY Edited by Professor Erwin."

Paragraph 3, sentence 1: "barracks" appeared as "barrack's."

Paragraph 6, sentence 2: "climbed" appeared as "climed."

Paragraph 7, sentence 9: "devilish" appeared as "devilsh."

Paragraph 8, sentence 1: "A silence hung" appeared as "A silence that hung."

Paragraph 9, sentence 4: "it's your neck" appeared as "its your neck."

Paragraph 11, sentence 2: "He gained speed" appeared as "He gained sped."

Paragraph 11, sentence 3: "though he had taken" appeared as "thought he had taken."

Paragraph 15, sentence 1: the original omitted the quotation marks before "thinks."

Paragraph 16, sentence 2: "edge" appeared as "elge."

Paragraph 18, sentence 3: Though the question mark ending this sentence could have been a typographical error in the original, it has been retained here.

Paragraph 18, sentence 15: "followed cautiously by" appeared as "following cautiously by," which idiom and paragraph 25 indicate is a typographical error; and "dogs meeting" appeared originally as "dogs meetin."

Paragraph 19, sentence 1: "C.O." appeared as "C.O"; and "three lesser lights" appeared as "thre lesser lights."

Paragraph 20: in the original a comma immediately followed the question mark.

Paragraph 21, sentence 1: " 'ere, sir" appeared as " 'ere sir."

Paragraph 23, sentence 1: the quotation marks preceding this sentence did not appear in the original.

Paragraph 28, sentence 1: the third set of quotation marks, being reversed in the original, erroneously closed a quotation instead of opening one.

Paragraph 33, sentence 1: the second set of quotation marks, being reversed in the original, erroneously opened a quotation instead of closing one.

Paragraph 35, sentence 1: the end of this sentence appeared without the question mark and closing quotation marks.

Paragraph 36, sentence 1: "he stared into" appeared as "he satred into."

Paragraph 36, sentences 2, 3, 4, and 5: Because the only available original text lacks the top of parts of these lines of type, this volume prints some of these letters without much textual justification and the quotation marks and the apostrophe without any textual justification whatever.

Paragraph 36, sentence 4: "N.C.O.'s" appeared as "N.C.O's."

Paragraph 39, sentence 4: "he was all staring eyes" appeared as "he was al lstaring eyes."

Paragraph 42, sentence 2: in the original this sentence did not begin with quotation marks.

Paragraph 50: in the original this sentence did not begin with quotation marks.

Paragraph 52, sentence 4: "You're" appeared as "Your'e."

Paragraph 52, sentence 5: "Why, I got" appeared as "Why I got."

Paragraph 54, sentence 1: the second set of quotation marks, being reversed in the original, erroneously opened a quotation instead of closing one.

Paragraph 55, sentence 5: double quotation marks appeared in the original before and after the letter "f."

"SAPPHICS.": *The Mississippian,* November 26, 1919, p. 3.

Line 4: the period which ends this line is an emendation, perhaps improper, of the comma which ended this line in *The Mississippian.*

Line 8: the comma which ends this line is an emendation, perhaps improper, of the period which ended this line in *The Mississippian.*

Line 23: "Lethean" appeared as "Lethan."

"AFTER FIFTY YEARS.": *The Mississippian,* December 10, 1919, p. 4.

Line 2: this reprinting, perhaps improperly, omits the period with which *The Mississippian* ended this line.

"UNE BALLADE DES FEMMES PERDUES": *The Mississippian,* January 28, 1920, p. 3.

Title: because of typographical error, this title appeared as "UNE BALAD HEDES FEMMES PERDUES" in *The Mississippian.*

The quotation from Villon: this appeared as " 'Mais ou sont les nieges d' antan' " in *The Mississippian.*

Line 4: *The Mississippian* printed "—Ca ne fait rein! Helas" as the first part of this line.

Line 6: in a holograph version of this poem dated January 1, 1920, in a decorated gift booklet, Faulkner hyphenated "lute strings" in line 6, "boarding school" in line 7, "love songs" in line 10, and "star dust" in line 20.

Line 9: "Amorous" appeared as "Amourous."

"NAIADS' SONG.": *The Mississippian,* February 4, 1920, p. 3.

Line 14: "there" appeared as "here."

Line 44: "glides he in forgetfulness" appeared as "glides he is forgetfulness."

"FANTOCHES.": *The Mississippian,* February 25, 1920, p. 3.
Title: in *The Mississippian,* presumably through typographical error, this title appeared as "FANTOUCHES."; because no such word seems to exist, this reprinting has changed the spelling to that of Verlaine's title.
"à Paul Verlaine.": the printer of *The Mississippian,* following his practice of using no accents, printed "a Paul Verlaine." here.
Line 1: this reprinting, perhaps improperly, retains *The Mississippian* spelling of "Scaramouches" and "Pucinella" on the ground that, though in Verlaine's poem, *"Fantoches,"* the first line (*"Scaramouche et Pulcinella,"*) uses the traditional spellings, Faulkner, who presumably changed one of these two traditional male figures into a woman, just possibly may have deliberately changed the traditional spelling of their names also.
Line 4: this reprinting, perhaps improperly, retains *The Mississippian* text's "of Bogona" on the ground that though "of Bologna" is the translation of Verlaine's *"Bolonais"* Faulkner may have altered this name deliberately just as he may have altered the poem's two other proper names (see note next above).
Line 5: "skull cap" appeared as "skull cup."
Line 6: "eye" appeared as "eyes."
Line 12: "garde" appeared as "grade."

"CLAIR DE LUNE.": *The Mississippian,* March 3, 1920, p. 6.
Line 4: "fanchise," which appeared in *The Mississippian,* is presumably a typographical error; if so, Faulkner may have written "franchise." But "franchise" fails to fit his otherwise rather regular rhyme scheme. Perhaps the reader would prefer to substitute here some such word as "fantasy."
Line 6: "conqueror" appeared as "conquerer."

"STREETS.": *The Mississippian,* March 17, 1920, p. 2.
Line 1: though *The Mississippian* ended the exclamation in this line and lines 13 and 17 with periods, it seems reason-

able to assume that the periods are typographical errors and should be replaced by exclamation points like those which end this same exclamation in lines 5 and 9 as well as in all its five appearances in Verlaine's poem.

Line 12: *The Mississippian* ended this line with a period which, correctly or not, is omitted in this reprinting on the assumption that it is a typographical error because all other lines in the poem except the five repetitions of the exclamation end without punctuation though some of them call for punctuation as much — or as little — as this line does.

"A POPLAR.": *The Mississippian,* March 17, 1920, p. 7.
Line 8: "ecstatic" appeared as "extatic."

"A CLYMENE.": *The Mississippian,* April 14, 1920, p. 3.
Title: following its practice of using no accents, *The Mississippian* printed this as "A CLYMENE."

"STUDY.": *The Mississippian,* April 21, 1920, p. 4.
Line 16: "silver" appeared as "silvtr."

"ALMA MATER.": *The Mississippian,* May 12, 1920, p. 3.
Line 14: in the original this line did not end with a period.

Drawing of four men facing the reader above the caption "CLASSES": *Ole Miss,* 1919-1920, Vol. XXIV, p. 29. Though this drawing is unsigned it is in the style characteristic of the four drawings Faulkner did sign in this volume of the annual.

Drawing of woman and man in high wind beneath the caption "Organizations": *Ole Miss,* 1919-1920, Vol. XXIV, p. 105.

Drawing of woman and army officer: *Ole Miss,* 1919-1920, Vol. XXIV, p. 145, on a page listing members of the A.E.F. Club.

Drawing of two men and a woman before candelabra beneath

the caption "Social Activities": *Ole Miss,* 1919-1920, Vol. XXIV, p. 155.

Drawing of woman and man dancing beside the caption "Red & Blue": *Ole Miss,* 1919-1920, Vol. XXIV, p. 157, on a page listing members of the Red and Blue Club, a dancing society.

"To a Co-ed": *Ole Miss,* 1919-1920, Vol. XXIV, p. 174.
Line 4: the original did not end this line with a period.

"BOOKS AND THINGS" [review of W. A. Percy, *In April Once*]: *The Mississippian,* November 10, 1920, p. 5.
Paragraph 2, sentence 1: "Mississippian, a graduate" appeared as "Mississippian a graduate."
Paragraphs 2 and 3: *The Mississippian,* printing several lines of type out of their proper order, put parts of each of these paragraphs in the other. The lines have been unscrambled here.
Paragraph 3, sentence 3: "His muse" appeared as "His His muse"; and "ecstasies" appeared as "ecstacies."
Paragraph 3, line 3 of the poem by Percy: *The Mississippian* did not end this line with Percy's comma.
Paragraph 3, line 8 of the poem by Percy: *The Mississippian* did not follow "alone" with Percy's comma.

"BOOKS & THINGS" [review of Conrad Aiken, *Turns and Movies*]: *The Mississippian,* February 16, 1921, p. 5.
The excerpt from Aiken's "Discordants": in *The Mississippian,* the fifth line did not end with Aiken's comma and in the seventh line his "belovèd" appeared as "beloved."

"CO-EDUCATION AT OLE MISS.": *The Mississippian,* May 4, 1921, p. 5.
Line 9: "lov'st" appeared as "love'st."

Drawing of sailor, soldier, and airman above the caption "FISH, FLESH, FOWL": *Ole Miss,* 1920-1921, Vol. XXV, p. 129, on a page listing members of the University's post of the American Legion.

Drawing of non-commissioned officer and four commissioned officers under the caption "A.E.F. CLUB": *Ole Miss,* 1920-1921, Vol. XXV, p. 131.

Decorative border and the caption "MARIONETTES": *Ole Miss,* 1920-1921, Vol. XXV, p. 135, on a page listing members of The Marionettes, a drama society. Though this drawing is unsigned it is in Faulkner's characteristic style.

Drawing of man and woman dancing before jazz orchestra: *Ole Miss,* 1920-1921, Vol. XXV, p. 137, on a page listing the members of the Red and Blue Club, a dancing society.

"NOCTURNE.": and decorative border: *Ole Miss,* 1920-1921, Vol. XXV, pp. 214-215. In *Ole Miss* the plates appeared in inverted order. Though this poem and drawing are unsigned they are in Faulkner's characteristic lettering and style.

"BOOKS & THINGS" [review of Edna St. Vincent Millay, *Aria da Capo*]: *The Mississippian,* January 13, 1922, p. 5.

"BOOKS & THINGS: AMERICAN DRAMA: EUGENE O'NEILL.": *The Mississippian,* February 3, 1922, p. 5.
Paragraph 1, sentence 2: "Rhone valley in the nineteenth century" appeared as "Rhone valley in the eighteenth century."
Paragraph 5, sentence 3: the quotation marks before the title "Gold" appeared as a single quotation mark.

"THE HILL": *The Mississippian,* March 10, 1922, pp. 1 and 2.
Paragraph 1, sentence 2: "invisibility" appeared as "invisability."
Paragraph 2: the end of this paragraph appeared without a period.
Paragraph 3, sentence 2: "simplicity of the court house columns was discolored" appeared as "simplicity of the court house columns were discolored."

Paragraph 4, sentence 3: "the tieless casual" appeared as "the Tieless casual."

Initials at the conclusion: though the original was without these initials, the next issue of *The Mississippian* (March 17, 1922, p. 5) printed this statement: "Correction: Through some error the initials 'W.F.' were omitted from the sketch entitled 'The Hill' which appeared in the last issue of The Mississippian. We hereby mak [*sic*] amends."

"BOOKS & THINGS: American Drama: Inhibitions": *The Mississippian,* March 17, 1922, p. 5; and March 24, 1922, p. 5.

Section 1, paragraph 1, sentence 1: "twenty-five" appeared as "twenty five."

Section 1, paragraph 1, sentence 2: "to Frank Crane's market" appeared as "to Frank Crane market," and "stratum" appeared as "strata."

Section 1, paragraph 2, sentence 3: "Kreymborg" appeared as "Kreyemborg."

Section 2, paragraph 2, sentence 3: "literary shibboleths and pogroms" appeared as "literary shibboleth and pogroms," with extra space after "shibboleth."

Section 2, paragraph 2: the March 17 installment ended with this paragraph.

Section 2, paragraph 3, sentence 5: ended in the original without a period.

Drawing of woman and man at rail of ship: *Ole Miss,* 1922, Vol. XXVI, p. 188, on a page listing the members of the French Club. Though this drawing and joke are unsigned they are in Faulkner's characteristic lettering and style.

"Portrait": *Double Dealer* (New Orleans), Vol. III (June, 1922), p. 337.

"BOOKS AND THINGS" [review of Joseph Hergesheimer, *Linda Condon, Cytherea,* and *The Bright Shawl*]: *The Mississippian,* December 15, 1922, p. 5.

Paragraph 2, sentence 3: "graceful" appeared as "fraceful."

Paragraph 3, sentence 2: "La figlia" appeared as "La figlio."

Paragraph 5, sentence 3: "skilful" appeared as "skilfull."

Drawing of three women boarding a streetcar while two men watch: *The Scream*, May, 1925, Vol. I, No. 5, p. 11. Later the plate was cut in two and used again, in *The Scream*, May, 1927, Vol. III, No. 8, where the section showing the three women appears on p. 12 and the section showing the two men appears on p. 14.

Drawing of one man supporting another before a statue: *The Scream*, May, 1925, Vol. I, No. 5, p. 14.

Drawing of two men and an automobile: *The Scream*, May, 1925, Vol. I, No. 5, p. 15.

APPENDIX

"On Criticism": *Double Dealer*, Vol. VII (January-February, 1925), pp. 83-84.
   Paragraph 1, sentence 6: "esprit de corps" appeared as "espirt-du-corps."
   Paragraph 4, sentence 4: "It's" appeared as "Its."
   Paragraph 10, sentence 4: "enough" appeared as "enought."

"Dying Gladiator": *Double Dealer*, Vol. VII (January-February, 1925), p. 85.

"Verse Old And Nascent: A Pilgrimage": *Double Dealer*, Vol. VII (April, 1925), pp. 129-131.
   Paragraph 4, sentence 4: "discriminating" appeared as "disciminating."
   Paragraph 10, sentence 1: "Spenser" appeared as "Spencer."
   Paragraph 10, sentence 4: "nightingale" appeared as "Nightingale."
   Paragraph 11, sentence 9: "Shelley" appeared as "Shelly."

"The Faun": *Double Dealer*, Vol. VII (April, 1925), p. 148.
   Line 13: "undreamt" appeared as "undreampt."

Drawing of an aviator hanging to an airplane by one hand: *The Scream*, 1925, Vol. II, No. 1, p. 12. This unsigned drawing, judging by its style and the styles of the drawings signed by other contributors to *The Scream*, possibly is by William Faulkner.